GUITAR LESSON
GOLDMINE

**AUDIO
ACCESS
INCLUDED**

100
CLASSICAL LESSONS

BY JULIE GOLDBERG & BURGESS SPEED

ISBN 978-1-4950-2008-7

HAL•LEONARD®
7777 W. BLUEMOUND RD. P.O. BOX 13819 MILWAUKEE, WI 53213

In Australia Contact:
Hal Leonard Australia Pty. Ltd.
4 Lentara Court
Cheltenham, Victoria, 3192 Australia
Email: ausadmin@halleonard.com.au

Visit Hal Leonard Online at
www.halleonard.com

CONTENTS

Lessons 1–50 by Burgess Speed

Lessons 51–100 by Julie Goldberg

Parts of a Classical Guitar

Before discussing the differences between classical and steel-string acoustics, let's look at a picture of a classical guitar with its various parts labeled.

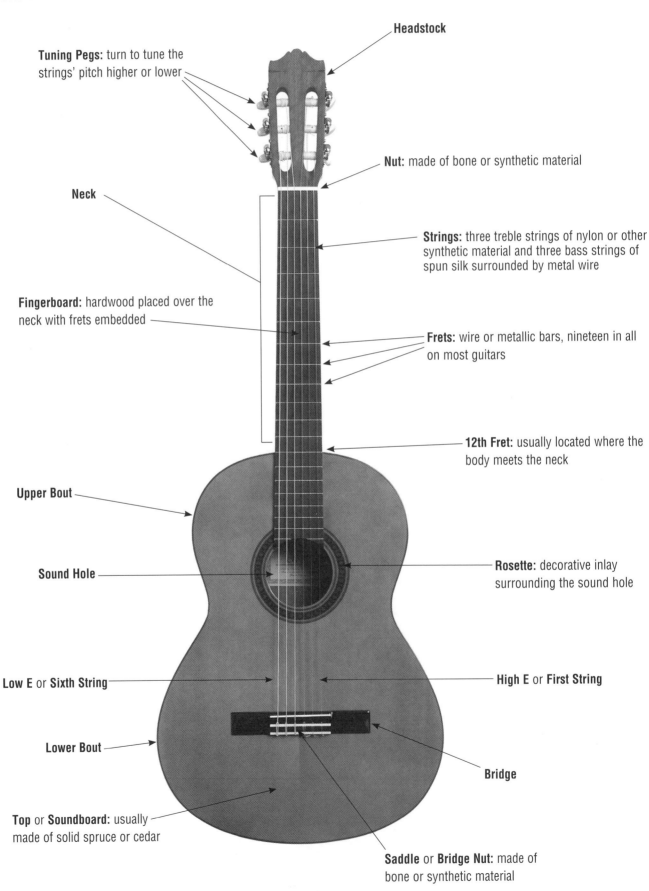

Headstock

Tuning Pegs: turn to tune the strings' pitch higher or lower

Neck

Nut: made of bone or synthetic material

Strings: three treble strings of nylon or other synthetic material and three bass strings of spun silk surrounded by metal wire

Fingerboard: hardwood placed over the neck with frets embedded

Frets: wire or metallic bars, nineteen in all on most guitars

12th Fret: usually located where the body meets the neck

Upper Bout

Sound Hole

Rosette: decorative inlay surrounding the sound hole

Low E or **Sixth String**

High E or **First String**

Lower Bout

Bridge

Top or **Soundboard:** usually made of solid spruce or cedar

Saddle or **Bridge Nut:** made of bone or synthetic material

The Differences

A classical guitar is actually an acoustic guitar (as opposed to electric), so what we are comparing here is a classical guitar, which has nylon strings, to a steel-string acoustic guitar.

TYPES OF MUSIC

Classical guitars are used for classical music and sometimes folk, while steel-string acoustic guitars are used for rock, blues, folk, country, and many other musical styles.

STRINGS

As mentioned above, classical guitars use nylon strings, while other acoustic guitars use steel strings. Nylon strings are thicker than steel strings and have a richer, mellower sound, as opposed to the bright, trebly twang of steel. On classical guitars, the strings are tied by hand at the bridge, while pegs, or bridge pins, are used to keep steel strings in place.

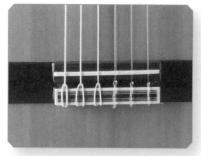

classical bridge

steel-string bridge

BODY

Below is a picture of a classical guitar beside a steel-string acoustic. Note the differences in body shape. The classical body is a bit smaller and has a more rounded feel. There are many variations in shape even among each type of guitar, but this visual comparison is a great starting point. Notice that the steel-string acoustic has a pickguard, or scratch plate—a black piece of plastic under the sound hole that protects the body's finish from being damaged by the pick. Finally, the body of the steel-string acoustic is braced for the high tension of steel strings. Classical guitars have much lighter bracing, so you would damage a classical guitar if you tried to string it with steel strings.

classical guitar

steel-string acoustic guitar

FINGERBOARD AND NECK

The fingerboard and neck on a classical guitar are wider than on a steel-string acoustic. This greater width accommodates the plucking of the fingers, whereas other acoustics have a narrower fingerboard more suitable to playing with a pick. Steel-string acoustics have fret markers (dots or some other design) usually at the third, fifth, seventh, ninth, 12th, 15th, and 17th frets; classical guitars have no fret markers.

Additionally, on a classical guitar, the neck joins the body at the 12th fret as opposed to the 14th fret like steel-string acoustics. Steel-string necks also have truss rods to adjust the curvature of the neck, while classical guitars do not.

HEADSTOCK

Classical guitars feature slotted headstocks with tuning pegs sticking out of the back. Steel-string acoustics have both slotted and solid headstocks. Slotted headstocks create more downward tension on the strings and are preferable to classical and fingerstyle players because of their great response and tone.

slotted headstock (classical)

solid headstock (steel-string acoustic)

LESSON #2: MUSIC READING—PITCH

Unless you play completely by ear, reading music is essential, especially for classical repertoire. Our lessons include both standard music notation and tablature (tab). The following is a quick tutorial on both. In this lesson, we will look specifically at reading *pitch*, the highness or lowness of a musical tone.

Staff, Clef, Measures, Bar Lines, Ledger Lines, and Repeat Signs

The standard notation *staff* consists of five lines. Guitar music is written in *treble clef*, also known as *G clef*. The clef appears at the beginning of every staff in a piece of music and encircles the line that represents the note G. Music is separated into *measures*, or *bars*, and is divided by *bar lines*. A *double bar line* marks the end of a section or short example, and a *terminal (final) bar line* marks the end of a piece.

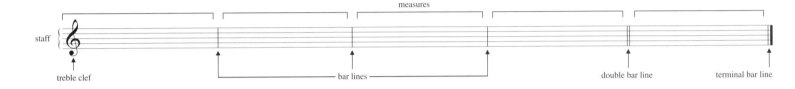

For pitches above or below the staff, *ledger lines* are used to extend the staff's range upward or downward. *Repeat signs* are used to indicate music that should be played more than once. When you see a *backward-facing repeat* only, it tells you to repeat from the beginning of the piece. When you see a backward-facing repeat and a *forward-facing repeat*, it tells you to go back and repeat from the forward-facing repeat sign.

Notes and Accidentals

The *music alphabet* consists of seven letters that repeat: A–B–C–D–E–F–G, A–B–C, etc. On the staff, both the lines and the spaces between the lines represent a letter of the music alphabet. A note's position on the staff determines the note's name.

Accidentals are signs that alter the pitch of a note. Below is a list of common accidentals.

Sharp (♯) = Raises the pitch of a note by one *half step* (one fret).

Flat (♭) = Lowers the pitch of a note by one half step.

Natural (♮) = Returns a note to its original pitch.

Double sharp (𝄪) = Raises the pitch of a note by one *whole step* (two frets).

Double flat (𝄫) = Lowers the pitch of a note by one whole step.

Dynamic Markings

Dynamics refer to how loudly or softly you play the music. The following is a common list of *dynamic markings* used in written music.

ppp = *Pianississimo* = Very, very soft

pp = *Pianissimo* = Very soft

p = *Piano* = Soft

mp = *Mezzo Piano* = Moderately soft

mf = *Mezzo Forte* = Moderately loud

f = *Forte* = Loud

ff = *Fortissimo* = Very loud

fff = *Fortississimo* = Very, very loud

‾‾‾◁ = Crescendo = Gradually louder

▷‾‾‾ = Decrescendo = Gradually softer

Tablature (Tab)

Tablature, or *tab*, is a sort of musical shorthand, and the usual presentation involves a tab staff directly under each standard notation staff for quick and easy reading.

The tab staff consists of six lines, each representing a guitar string. The highest line is the first string (high E) and the lowest line is the sixth string (low E). Numbers on the lines tell you what frets to press on which strings. Check out the following example:

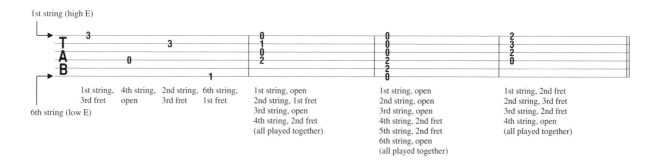

Tab provides a quick way to see the exact location of notes in an arrangement, but it does have some limitations. For rhythm, note values, and fretting-hand fingerings, you will need to refer to the corresponding standard notation. However, tab is a great jump-starter to learning a piece, especially if your standard notation skills are not that strong.

LESSON #3: MUSIC READING—TIME

The following is a quick tutorial on an essential aspect of reading music: time. Music is felt in *beats*, which is like a pulse, or musical heartbeat. Measures divide music into small groups of beats (1, 2, 3, 4; 1, 2, 3, 4, etc.). The organization of music in time is known as *rhythm*, and any measure can have a different rhythm, or combination of notes and/or *rests* (silences).

Parts of a Note, Note Values, and Rest Values

The length, or *value*, of a note (how long it rings out) is indicated by the appearance of the note, so let's start by looking at the different parts of a note. Some notes have solid noteheads, some have hollow noteheads, some have stems, some have flags, and some have multiple flags.

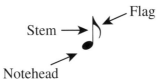

Now, let's look at the different types of notes and note values and how they relate to each other.

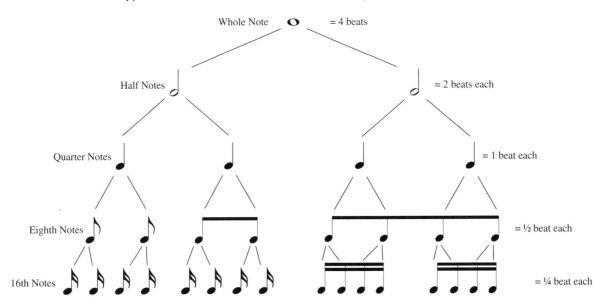

For every note, there is a corresponding rest. Below, you can see the different rests and rest values and how they correspond to each other.

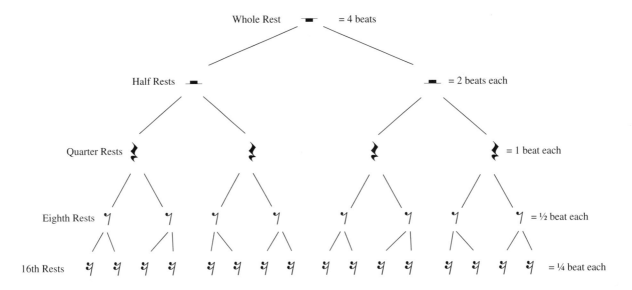

Ties and Dots

A *tie* is a curved line that connects two notes of the same pitch, extending the value of the first note by the value of the second note (the two notes are added together). For instance, a half note (two beats) tied to a quarter note (one beat) lasts for three beats.

When a *dot* is placed to the right of a note or rest, it extends the note's or rest's duration by one half of its original value. For example, a dotted quarter note equals one-and-a-half beats ($1 + \frac{1}{2} = 1\frac{1}{2}$). This can also be viewed as a quarter note tied to an eighth note (see below).

Time Signatures

A *time signature* appears at the beginning of a piece of music and indicates how many beats are in each measure (the top number) and what type of note equals one beat (the bottom number).

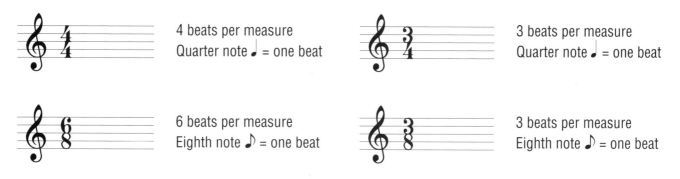

4 beats per measure
Quarter note = one beat

3 beats per measure
Quarter note = one beat

6 beats per measure
Eighth note = one beat

3 beats per measure
Eighth note = one beat

Tempo Markings

Tempo refers to the speed, or pace, of the music. The following is a list of common tempo markings, all of which feature Italian terms.

Lento = Slow
Adagio = Moderately slow, stately
Andante = At a walking pace
Andantino = Slightly faster than andante
Moderato = Moderately
Allegretto = Moderately fast
Allegro = Fast, lively, and bright
Vivace = Quick
Presto = Extremely fast
Prestissimo = Faster than presto; as fast as possible

Tempo is also indicated with *metronome markings* like the following:

♩ = 80

This means that there are 80 quarter-note beats per minute (BPM).

LESSON #4: FINGERNAIL MAINTENANCE

Some classical guitarists pluck with only the flesh of their fingertips; however, a majority of players use a combination of flesh and fingernail. Flesh-only produces a mellow tone, while well-shaped and maintained fingernails provide more volume and wider variations in tone. (As a side note, the fingernails of your *fretting hand* should be as short as possible so that they don't interfere when pressing the strings against the frets.)

Length

The optimum fingernail length may vary from player to player, but the following instructions give you a perfect place to start:

1. Hold your plucking hand up, with fingers at eye level and palm toward your face.

2. Look at the index (*i*), middle (*m*), and ring (*a*) fingers. If you cannot see any nail, it's too short (see Photo 1). If you see more than just a little nail, it's too long (see Photo 2). If the nail is just peeking over the crescent of each fingertip, it's the right length (see Photo 3).

3. Turn the pad of your thumb toward you. The same guidelines that apply to your other three fingers also apply to the thumb; however, the thumbnail can be slightly longer than the other fingernails (see Photo 4).

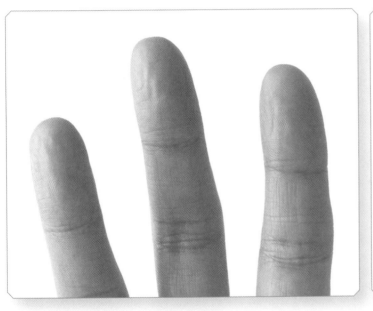

1: too short

2: too long

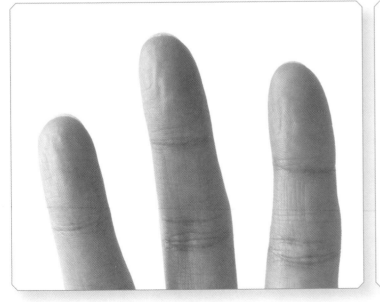

3: just right

4: just right

Shaping

Your fingernails should be shaped like a ramp sloping toward the string. This allows for a smooth plucking motion, whereby the fingernail sweeps across the string and then releases it with the most efficient movement and cleanest tone.

When first shaping your nails, or if you haven't played classical guitar in a while, use the rougher side of an emery board to achieve the desired contour, gradually switching to smoother grit. Four-way all-purpose nail files and buffers are great for this purpose (see photo below).

four-way all-purpose nail file/buffer

When filing your fingernails, the board should be held flat under the nail, with the nail facing upward. Move your finger back and forth across the board to achieve the desired shape, turning your finger as if against a lathe, and sometimes gently knocking off excess nail with the buffer or other fine-grit section of the file.

Buffing

When the nails are in shape, polish them with the finest finish on the buffer. You do not want any burs or imperfections on the nail, as these will produce scratches and defects in your tone—and will hinder good plucking motion. Buff the top-ends, bottom-ends, and sides to achieve as perfect a nail as possible.

Keep files and buffers in your guitar case because you need to buff your fingernails prior to every practice session or performance. This may seem like a burden, but it only takes a minute or two (if the nails are already shaped)—and the clean tone and ease of playing are well worth it!

Some Additional Thoughts

It's easy for a professional guitarist to maintain nails, but maybe not so easy for players with other professions. If you simply cannot grow good nails, you can try false ones. There are many false fingernail products on the market specifically intended for guitar players.

Also, if your nails crack and chip easily, you can try nail hardener, another product easily obtained in stores and online. Nail hardener is great to use, especially preceding a performance, recording session, or other event where you want to ensure the strength and integrity of your nails. Remember: if your nails are "off," there's a good chance your performance will be off, as well!

LESSON #5: THE CHROMATIC SCALE

The music alphabet consists of all the natural notes: A, B, C, D, E, F, and G. When we add the notes in between the natural notes, using sharps and flats, we get all the notes on the guitar fretboard:

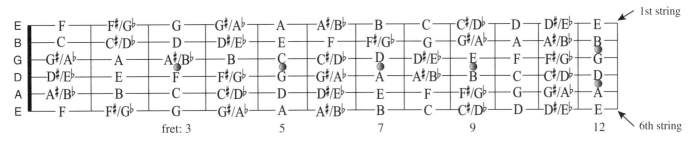

Notice that some notes have both a sharp name and a flat name. For instance, the note on the second fret of the first string can be called either F♯ or G♭. When notes have the same exact pitch but different names, they are *enharmonic equivalents*; F♯ and G♭ are enharmonic equivalents.

There are 12 half steps in an *octave*; therefore, there are 12 possible notes in an octave. (An octave is the distance between two notes of the same name.) These notes are known as the *chromatic scale*.

The chromatic scale can use sharp notes when ascending and flat notes when descending. If we start with the first letter of the music alphabet, the chromatic scale would be A–A♯–B–C–C♯–D–D♯–E–F–F♯–G–G♯ when ascending, and A–A♭–G–G♭–F–E–E♭–D–D♭–C–B–B♭ when descending. Let's look at the A chromatic scale on a single string—the fifth string.

A CHROMATIC SCALE (SINGLE STRING)

You can start the chromatic scale from any note. Let's check out the E chromatic scale on the low E string.

E CHROMATIC SCALE (SINGLE STRING)

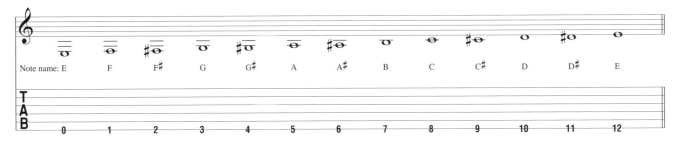

The following is a two-octave E chromatic scale in open position. Fret the notes on the first fret with the first finger, the notes on the second fret with the second finger, the notes on the third fret with the third finger, and the notes on the fourth fret with the fourth finger. Of course, the open strings do not require a fretting-hand finger. In addition, alternate between the index (*i*) and middle (*m*) fingers of the plucking hand.

TWO-OCTAVE E CHROMATIC SCALE (OPEN POSITION)

You can use the scale above as a warmup, but the following example is perhaps better for that purpose because it requires little thought and therefore forces you to concentrate on technique. This is sometimes referred to as the "Spider Exercise" because of the way the fretting-hand fingers crawl across the fretboard.

The Spider Exercise is *semi*-chromatic because it skips a half step in most instances when changing to the next string. In terms of fretting-hand fingers, you will use a 1–2–3–4, 1–2–3–4 pattern from the sixth string to the first string. Then, you will shift to the position a half step higher and descend with a 4–3–2–1, 4–3–2–1 pattern from the first string to the sixth.

(**Note:** Positions are indicated with Roman numerals: I = first position, II = second position, etc.). When you get to the bottom note, shift up to the position a half step higher and repeat the process. Go as high as you can on the fretboard, repeating the pattern. Concentrate on good fretting- and plucking-hand technique. With the plucking hand, alternate between *i* and *m* until you get the hang of all the notes, then alternate between *m* and *a* (ring), and *i* and *a*.

THE SPIDER EXERCISE

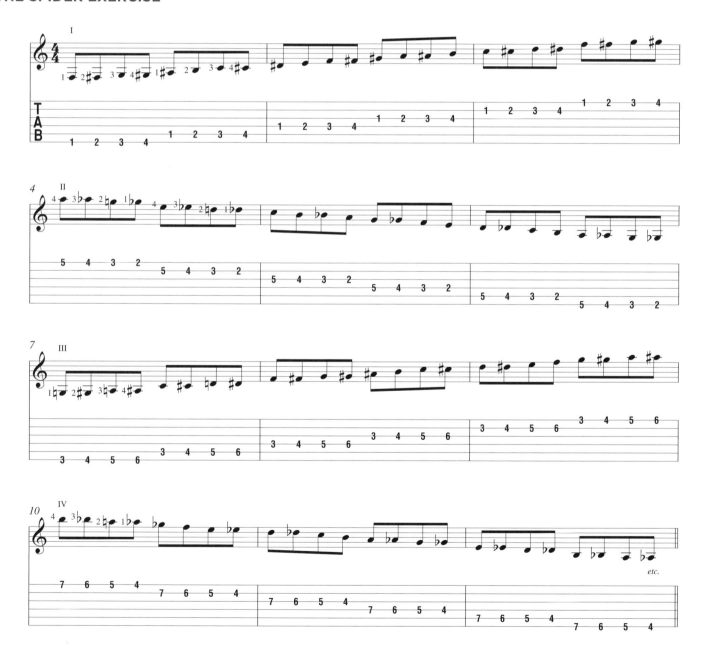

LESSON #6: NATURAL NOTES IN OPEN POSITION

The *music alphabet* consists of seven note names: A–B–C–D–E–F–G. After G, it goes back to A and repeats. For example: C–D–E–F–G–A–B–C–D–E–F–G–A–B.

The notes of the music alphabet are the *natural notes*, which means they are not altered by sharps or flats. On a piano keyboard, the natural notes are all of the white keys. The guitar fretboard is arranged in *half-step* increments; that is, one fret equals one half step. Two frets equal a *whole step*. Each pair of consecutive natural notes is a whole step apart, except for B–C and E–F. Below is a diagram showing the natural notes on a guitar fretboard up to the 12th fret.

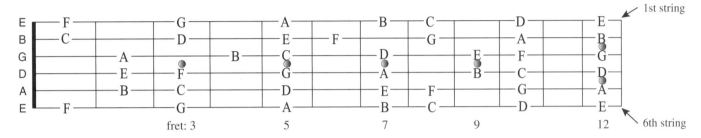

You can follow the preceding diagram and play the natural notes on each string, or you can apply the music alphabet and the whole-step/half-step principle mentioned above and figure out the notes for yourself. Either way, you should eventually make yourself familiar with all these notes. For now, we will concern ourselves only with the notes in open position. Below, you will see the notes in standard notation and tab.

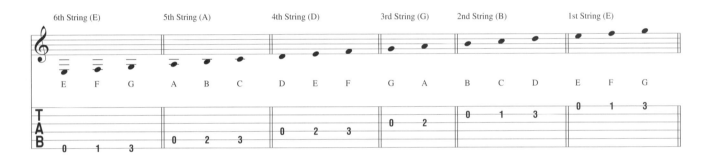

Let's play these notes in various combinations. For now, all notes should be plucked with the *i* and *m* (index and middle) fingers, though it is standard practice to pluck strings 4–6 with the thumb.

EXAMPLE 1: ASCENDING AND DESCENDING

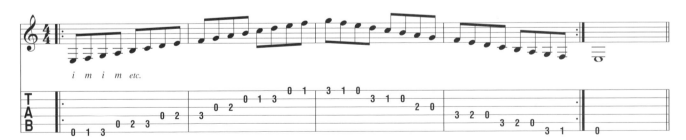

EXAMPLE 2: STRING 1

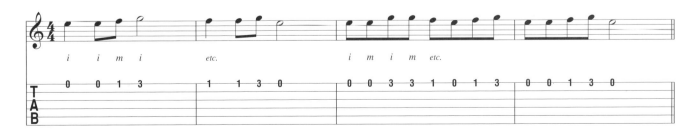

EXAMPLE 3: STRINGS 1 AND 2 (EXCERPT FROM "ODE TO JOY" BY LUDWIG VAN BEETHOVEN)

EXAMPLE 4: STRINGS 1–4

EXAMPLE 5: STRINGS 1–5

EXAMPLE 6: STRINGS 1–6

LESSON #7: ACCIDENTALS IN OPEN POSITION

This lesson will get you accustomed to reading and playing accidentals—sharps, flats, and naturals—in open position. You may not always come across the abundance of accidentals that you see in this lesson but, by immersing yourself in them, you will be able to read most beginner and intermediate pieces more easily.

Accidentals only last for the measure in which they are indicated. For instance, if there is an F♯ in measure 2 of an example, the next F you encounter, even if it is the first note in measure 3, would be an F *natural*. A natural sign is not needed in this case; however, courtesy accidentals (often enclosed in parentheses) can be used to remind the player how a note is supposed to be played. So, in the case just mentioned, the F in measure 3 would appear with a ♮ in front of it.

Example 1 features a melody on strings 1 and 2. In this lesson, we will supply some courtesy accidentals—but remember: as the name implies, this is a courtesy, so you may not see them in other pieces or examples.

EXAMPLE 1: STRINGS 1–2

Example 2 features natural notes and accidentals on strings 1–4. The melody may sound a little strange, but the point of these exercises is to throw you headfirst into reading a variety of accidentals.

EXAMPLE 2: STRINGS 1–4

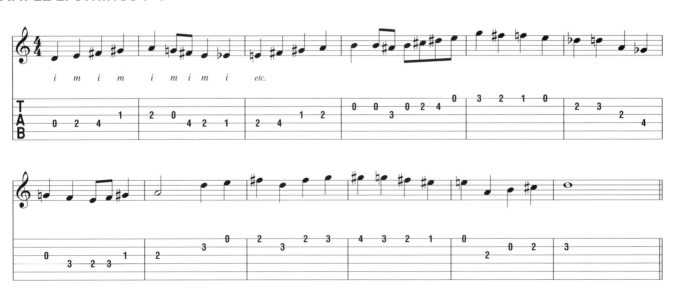

Closing this lesson is an exercise by guitarist and composer Matteo Carcassi. Exercise 3 features natural notes and accidentals on all six strings. Again, the melody may sound a little strange, but if you can read and play the examples in this lesson, you will have a strong foundation for moving on to other techniques and a greater musical variety.

LESSON #8: MAJOR SCALE THEORY

A *scale* is a series of notes in a particular arrangement of *half steps* (one fret) and *whole steps* (two frets). There are many different types of scales, the most important of which, at least in terms of music theory, is the *major scale*. All other scales can be defined by comparing them to the major scale.

The major scale has a very recognizable sound and is often identified by the *solfège* syllables: Do–Re–Mi–Fa–Sol–La–Ti–Do. Notice there are seven syllables (the first is repeated at the end)—the major scale contains seven notes that can be expressed with solfège or indicated with numbers known as *scale degrees* (1–2–3–4–5–6–7–8). (**Note:** Scale degree 8 is the *octave* of scale degree 1.) The first note of the scale, the note upon which the scale is built, is the *tonic*. The note names always cycle consecutively through the *music alphabet* (A–B–C–D–E–F–G), depending on which letter you start with; for example, the C major scale would be C–D–E–F–G–A–B–C.

Below is the C major scale, which has no sharps or flats. The note names and scale degrees are indicated.

C MAJOR SCALE

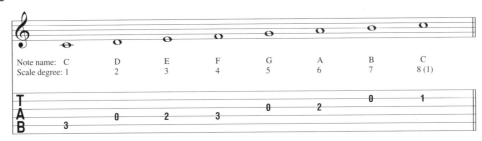

The Major Scale Formula

Every major scale is constructed from the same formula of whole steps and half steps. In the example below, you will see that this formula is: whole–whole–half–whole–whole–whole–half. We'll use "W" to indicate whole step and "H" to indicate half step.

C MAJOR SCALE

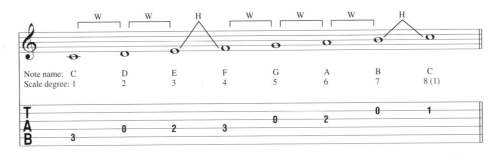

If we start from any note and follow the major scale formula above, the result will be another major scale whose letter name is the same as the starting note. Some scales will require sharps to maintain the scale formula, and some will require flats. Let's look at some examples.

If we start with a G note and make our way through the music alphabet, we get the following:

G MAJOR SCALE

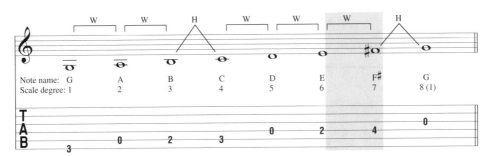

Notice in the previous figure that, in order to maintain the required whole step between E and F♯, we needed to sharp (raise) the F.

Let's look at another scale that uses sharps to maintain the major scale formula. This one starts with a D note and requires us to sharp the F and C notes to maintain the pattern.

D MAJOR SCALE

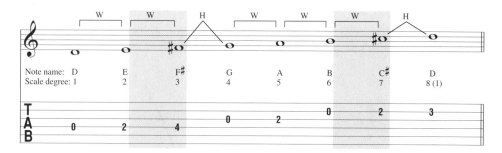

Below is a major scale built on the note F. Notice that we had to flat (lower) the B to preserve the half step between the third and fourth scale degrees.

F MAJOR SCALE

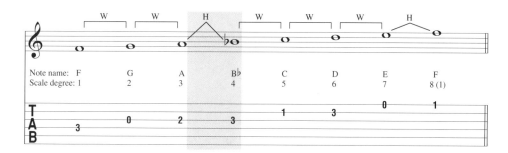

We'll look at one more, this time with a B♭ tonic. Coincidentally, we need to flat the fourth scale degree for this one, as well.

B♭ MAJOR SCALE

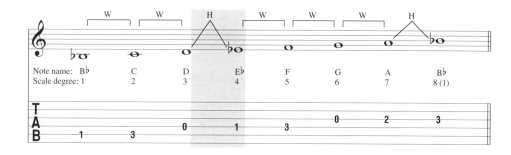

Because there are 12 possible notes (15 if you count the enharmonic equivalents), there are 12 major scales: C, G, D, A, E, B, F, B♭, E♭, A♭, D♭, and G♭.

LESSON #9: MINOR SCALE THEORY

Relative Minor

Every major scale has a *relative minor*, which is built on the sixth degree of the major scale. What this means is that the relative major and minor share the same key signature; the same notes are used as well, just starting and ending in a different place. So, if we were to look at the C major scale and start and end on the sixth scale degree, A, we would have the A minor scale, which is the relative minor of C major.

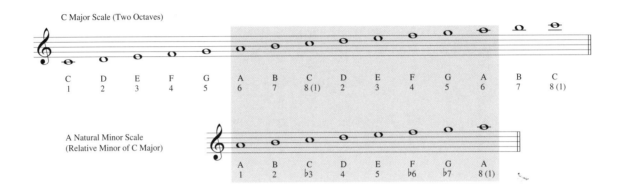

There are three types of minor scales: *natural minor, harmonic minor*, and *melodic minor*. Let's look at all three.

Natural Minor

As illustrated above, when you start and end with the sixth scale degree of any major scale, the result is a natural minor scale. The formula in scale degrees is: 1–2–♭3–4–5–♭6–♭7–8. (**Note:** Any time a scale degree is lowered or raised when compared to the degrees of a major scale, a flat or sharp appears before it.) The natural minor scale has its own step formula, as well: whole–half–whole–whole–half–whole–whole.

A NATURAL MINOR SCALE

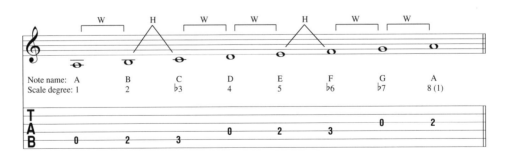

Harmonic Minor

The harmonic minor scale has a more exotic sound and is often used to *harmonize* music (i.e., compose chords and/or accompaniment) in minor keys. To create a harmonic minor scale, start with a natural minor scale and raise the seventh degree (this becomes a natural 7th). The formula in scale degrees is: 1–2–♭3–4–5–♭6–7. The step formula for the harmonic minor scale is: whole–half–whole–whole–half–whole+half–half.

A HARMONIC MINOR SCALE

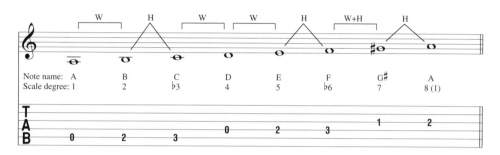

Melodic Minor

The melodic minor scale is often used to create melodies. It is unique in that it is different when ascending and descending. The ascending form is like the natural minor scale but with a natural 6th and natural 7th (this can also be thought of as being like the major scale but with a ♭3rd). The descending form is exactly like the natural minor scale. So, the scale degrees for the ascending form are: 1–2–♭3–4–5–6–7. The step formula for the ascending form is: whole–half–whole–whole–whole–whole–half.

A MELODIC MINOR SCALE

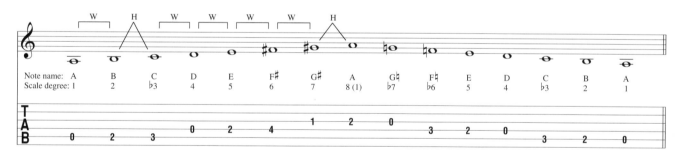

A Note About Minor Keys

A minor key usually indicates the presence of the harmonic minor or melodic minor scale. The reason for this is that traditional theory necessitates the presence of a *leading tone* (the natural 7th) to have a true "key." When the natural minor is used to create melodies, it is considered a *mode* (the natural minor scale being the sixth mode—the *Aeolian* mode—of the major scale).

So, when referencing the relative minor key, you will most likely be referring to a tonal structure using either the harmonic minor or melodic minor scale.

LESSON #10: KEY SIGNATURES

Keys

A *key* is the tonal center of a piece of music. The notes of a major scale make up the notes of a major key with the same name. Both the scale and the key are named for the tonic note. For instance, the notes of the C major scale constitute the key of C major. There are no sharps or flats in the C major scale, so there are no sharps or flats in the key of C major, or simply, the "key of C." Additionally, keys can be major or minor.

Key Signatures

A *key signature* is located at the beginning of every piece of music and indicates the key by showing how many sharps or flats are in the piece. For example, let's look at the A major scale.

Instead of inserting a sharp to the left of every C, F, and G note, a key signature is used.

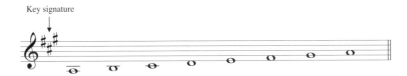

The accidentals in the key signature remain in effect throughout the piece unless altered by a natural sign ♮.

Below are all of the major key signatures, with their relative minor keys indicated, as well. Remember: the key of C major (and its relative, A minor) has no sharps or flats.

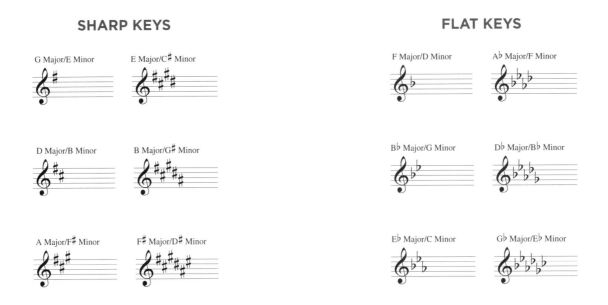

TIPS FOR FIGURING OUT WHAT KEY YOU'RE IN

▶ **For sharp keys:** Take the last sharp, the one all the way to the right, raise it a half step, and that is your key. For instance, look at the key signature with three sharps. The sharp all the way to the right is G♯. Raise G♯ a half step and you get A. So, the key with three sharps is A major.

▶ **For flat keys:** First, you need to remember that the key of F has one flat, B♭. But after that, it's easy to figure out the flat keys. The second-to-last flat tells you the key. For example, if you look at the key with five flats, you'll see that the second-to-last flat is D♭. Thus, the key with five flats is the key of D♭ major.

▶ **Major or minor:** To determine if you are in a major or minor key, you would first look at the key signature, which tells you that you are in one of two keys—the major or its relative minor. Next, you need to look at the music. Generally, if you are starting and ending on the tonic of the major scale, you are in the major key. If you are starting and ending on the tonic of the minor scale, you are in the relative minor key. For instance, if a piece of music has one sharp, it is either in the key of G major or E minor. If the piece starts and ends with an E minor chord, it is safe to say that the piece is in the key of E minor.

The good news is, you won't come across *all* of these keys when playing classical guitar, but eventually, you will become acquainted with many of them.

Circle of 5ths

A helpful system for organizing and remembering keys and key signatures is the *circle of 5ths*. (**Note:** A *5th* is the distance between the tonic and the fifth degree of a scale.) Check out the following diagram:

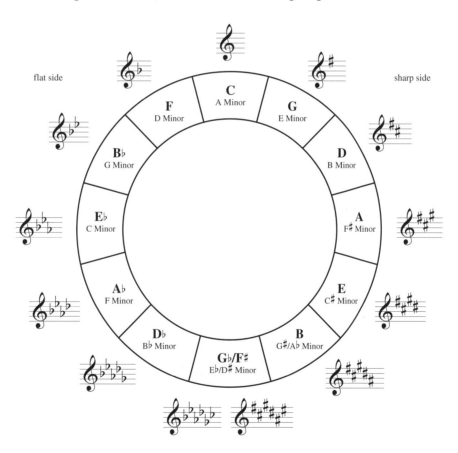

At the top of the circle of 5ths is C major (A minor), which has no sharps or flats. From that point, if we travel clockwise around the circle, we get the sharp keys. If we go up a 5th from C, we get G. If we go up a 5th from G, we get D, etc. Each time we go up a 5th, we add a sharp to the key signature, and that sharp is always the 7th of that key.

If we start from C and proceed counterclockwise around the circle, we get the flat keys. However, in this direction, each new key is a 4th higher than the previous one. From C to F is a 4th, from F to B♭ is a 4th, etc. In this direction, we add a flat to each new key signature, and that flat is always the 4th of that key.

Note that G♭ and F♯ occupy the same point of the circle. This means they are *enharmonic equivalents*—the pitches are exactly the same in both keys, but they are spelled with different note names.

It is extremely important for classical guitarists to know their scales. Not only do they provide the tonal context for a piece of music, but they also present excellent opportunities for developing technique, dexterity, and speed.

Below, we'll look at all the major scales with sharp keys. To do this, we'll go clockwise around the circle of 5ths, starting with C major (which has no sharps or flats). In other words, our first tonic will be C, then we'll go up a 5th to G, then to D, A, E, and B. Each time we go up, we will add a sharp to the key signature, just as with the circle of 5ths.

Open-Position Fingerings

The scales in this lesson are in open position, which can be synonymous with first position. In both open position and first position, the first finger is assigned to the first fret, the second finger to the second fret, the third finger to the third fret, and the fourth finger to the fourth fret (sometimes extending up to the fifth fret). The difference between "open" position and "first" position is that open position utilizes open strings.

It is valuable to know all of the notes of a scale in a given position—not just a one- or two-octave fingering. The scales here comprise all of the notes of the indicated keys in open position. Some of these scales may be more common than others, but it is essential for you to know them all.

Practice Tips and Right-Hand Fingering

The following are some tips to help you master the major scales in this lesson.

▶ Learn one scale at a time, practicing slowly until the fingering becomes comfortable.

▶ Incorporate the new scale into your daily warmup routine.

▶ Memorize the scale. You should be able to play the scale as if it were second nature.

▶ Use a metronome or some other time-keeping device, gradually increasing your tempo.

▶ Always strive for a full, crisp tone across all the notes.

▶ Each time you practice a scale, go through the plucking-hand fingerings below:

- *i–m–i–m–i–m*, etc.

- *im–im–im–im*, etc. (doubling each note)

- *m–a–m–a–m–a*, etc.

- *ma–ma–ma–ma*, etc.

- *i–a–i–a–i–a*, etc.

- *ia–ia–ia–ia*, etc.

C MAJOR SCALE

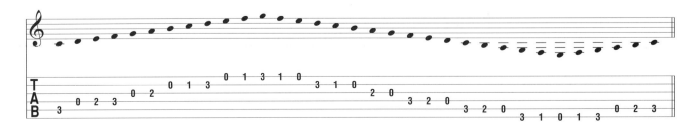

G MAJOR SCALE

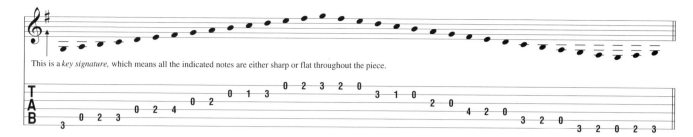

This is a *key signature,* which means all the indicated notes are either sharp or flat throughout the piece.

D MAJOR SCALE

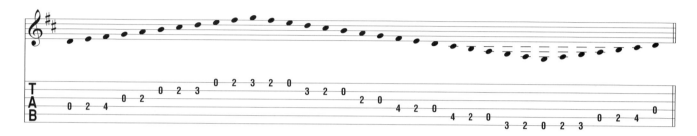

A MAJOR SCALE

E MAJOR SCALE

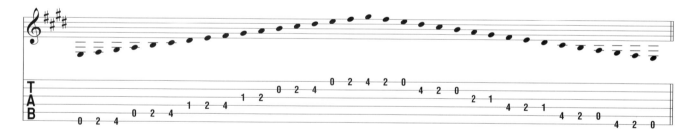

B MAJOR SCALE

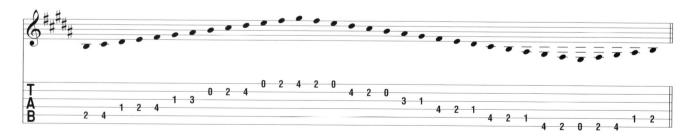

LESSON #12: MAJOR SCALES, PART 2

Let's look at all the major scales with flat keys. To do this, we'll go counterclockwise around the circle of 5ths, starting with F major (which has one flat). When you travel clockwise around the circle, your tonic notes ascend in 5ths. However, when you proceed around the circle in a counterclockwise direction, your tonic notes ascend in 4ths. So, our first tonic will be F, then we'll go up a 4th to B♭, then to E♭, A♭, D♭, and G♭. Each time we go up, we will add a flat to the key signature, just as we do for the circle of 5ths.

Some of the flat keys are more or less common to classical guitar music, while others are not so common. For instance, you will come across F and B♭ major more often than D♭ and G♭. In general, the sharp keys are more widely used than the flat keys.

Open-Position Fingerings

The following scales are in open position, with the exception of D♭ major, which includes no open strings. Because of this, the D♭ major scale can just be referred to as being in first position. In both open and first positions, the first finger is assigned to the first fret, the second finger to the second fret, the third finger to the third fret, and the fourth finger to the fourth fret (sometimes extending up to the fifth fret). A couple of these scales feature only one open string (A♭ major and G♭ major), one of them features two open strings (E♭ major), one features three open strings (B♭ major), and one features five open strings (F major).

It is important to know that the fingerings for open-position scales cannot be moved to different areas of the fretboard and, thereby, *transposed* to other keys. However, a scale that has no open strings, like D♭ major, is *movable*, which means it can be transposed by simply moving the entire scale fingering to a different fret. For example, if we were to start the D♭ scale fingering at the fifth fret (D) instead of the fourth, and follow the same fingering pattern, the result would be the D major scale.

It is valuable to know all of the notes of a scale in a given position. The following scales comprise all of the notes of the indicated keys in open (and, in the case of D♭, first) position.

Practice Tips and Right-Hand Fingering

The following are some tips to help you master the major scales in this lesson.

▶ Learn one scale at a time, practicing slowly until the fingering becomes comfortable.

▶ Incorporate the new scale into your daily warmup routine.

▶ Memorize the scale. You should be able to play the scale as if it were second nature.

▶ Use a metronome or some other time-keeping device, gradually increasing your tempo.

▶ Always strive for a full, crisp tone across all the notes.

▶ Each time you practice a scale, go through the plucking-hand fingerings below:

- *i–m–i–m–i–m,* etc.

- *im–im–im–im,* etc. (doubling each note)

- *m–a–m–a–m–a,* etc.

- *ma–ma–ma–ma,* etc.

- *i–a–i–a–i–a,* etc.

- *ia–ia–ia–ia,* etc.

F MAJOR SCALE

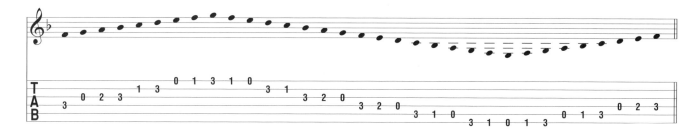

B♭ MAJOR SCALE

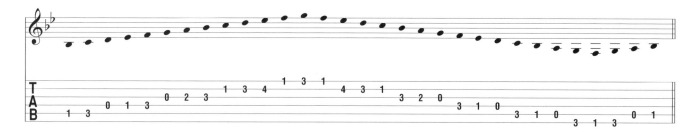

E♭ MAJOR SCALE

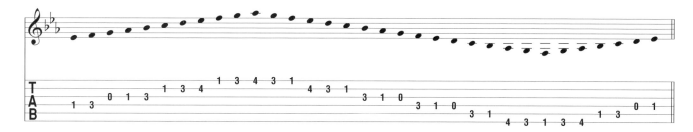

A♭ MAJOR SCALE

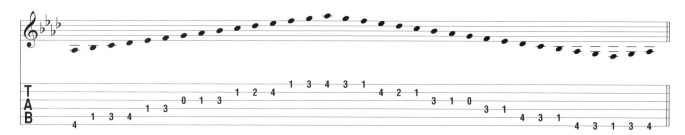

D♭ MAJOR SCALE

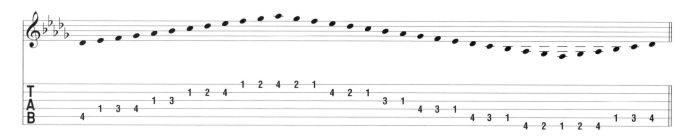

G♭ MAJOR SCALE

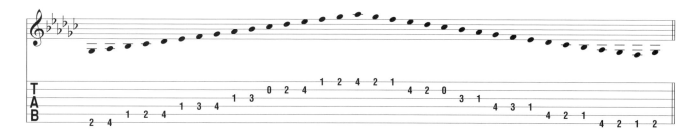

LESSON #13: MINOR SCALES, PART 1

In this lesson, we'll look at minor scales with sharp keys. Specifically, we'll look at melodic minor scales, because they are the minor-scale type typically used to create melodies in classical music. The melodic minor scale is like a natural minor scale but with raised sixth and seventh tones when ascending, and when descending, it is exactly like the natural minor scale. Because melodic minor has two forms—one when going up and one when going down—it can be tricky to remember.

We'll go clockwise around the circle of 5ths, starting with A minor. Then, we'll go up a 5th to E minor, then to B minor, F♯ minor, C♯ minor, and G♯ minor. Each time we go up, we will add a sharp to the key signature, just as with the circle of 5ths. Also, to accommodate the formula for the melodic minor scale, there will be additional accidentals in the scales themselves.

Open-Position Fingerings

The scales in this lesson are in open position, with one reach up to the fifth fret (with the pinky) in the A melodic minor scale. The following fingerings comprise all the notes of the indicated keys in open position. Some of these scales may be more common than others, but it is important to know them all.

Practice Tips and Right-Hand Fingering

The following are some tips to help you master the minor scales in this lesson.

▶ Learn one scale at a time, practicing slowly until the fingering becomes comfortable.

▶ Incorporate the new scale into your daily warmup routine.

▶ Memorize the scale. You should be able to play the scale as if it were second nature.

▶ Use a metronome or some other time-keeping device, gradually increasing your tempo.

▶ Always strive for a full, crisp tone across all the notes.

▶ Each time you practice a scale, go through the plucking-hand fingerings below:

- *i–m–i–m–i–m,* etc.

- *im–im–im–im,* etc. (doubling each note)

- *m–a–m–a–m–a,* etc.

- *ma–ma–ma–ma,* etc.

- *i–a–i–a–i–a,* etc.

- *ia–ia–ia–ia,* etc.

A MELODIC MINOR SCALE

E MELODIC MINOR SCALE

B MELODIC MINOR SCALE

F# MELODIC MINOR SCALE

C# MELODIC MINOR SCALE

G# MELODIC MINOR SCALE

LESSON #14: MINOR SCALES, PART 2

In this lesson, we'll look at minor scales with flat keys. Specifically, we'll look at melodic minor scales, because they are the minor-scale type typically used to create melodies in classical music. The melodic minor scale is like a natural minor scale but with raised sixth and seventh tones when ascending, and when descending, it is exactly like the natural minor scale. Because the melodic minor has two forms—one when going up and one when going down—it can be a challenge to remember.

We'll go counterclockwise around the circle of 5ths, starting with D minor (which has one flat). Then, we'll go up a 4th to G minor, then to C minor, F minor, Bb minor, and Eb minor. Each time we go up, we will add a flat to the key signature, just as with the circle of 5ths. Also, to accommodate the formula for the melodic minor scale, there will be additional accidentals in the scales themselves.

Open-Position Fingerings

The scale fingerings in this lesson comprise all the notes in open position for the indicated keys. Some of these scales may be more common than others, but it is important to know them all.

Practice Tips and Right-Hand Fingering

The following are some tips to help you master the minor scales in this lesson.

▶ Learn one scale at a time, practicing slowly until the fingering becomes comfortable.

▶ Incorporate the new scale into your daily warmup routine.

▶ Memorize the scale. You should be able to play the scale as if it were second nature.

▶ Use a metronome or some other time-keeping device, gradually increasing your tempo.

▶ Always strive for a full, crisp tone across all the notes.

▶ Each time you practice a scale, go through the plucking-hand fingerings below:

- *i–m–i–m–i–m*, etc.

- *im–im–im–im*, etc. (doubling each note)

- *m–a–m–a–m–a*, etc.

- *ma–ma–ma–ma*, etc.

- *i–a–i–a–i–a*, etc.

- *ia–ia–ia–ia*, etc.

D MELODIC MINOR SCALE

G MELODIC MINOR SCALE

C MELODIC MINOR SCALE

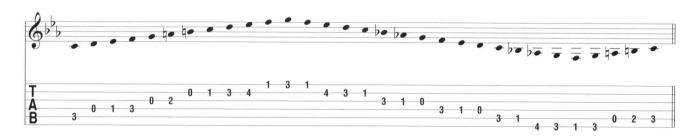

F MELODIC MINOR SCALE

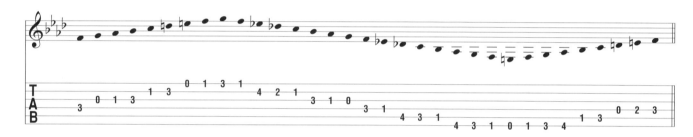

Bb MELODIC MINOR SCALE

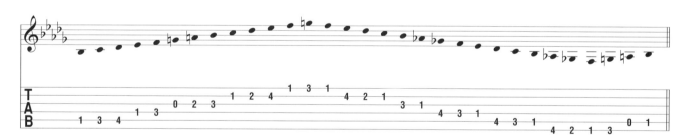

Eb MELODIC MINOR SCALE

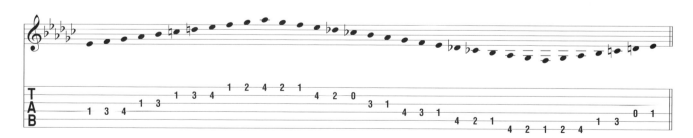

LESSON #15: SINGLE-NOTE MELODIES

This lesson is intended to provide more practice with single-note melodies in open position. Strive for a good tone on both pieces.

Practice and Performance Tips: Besard

Our first piece is an arrangement of an early 17th-century lute piece by Jean Baptiste Besard.

▶ The tempo is *moderato* and should be played at about 110 bpm.

▶ Try using rest strokes on the downbeat of each measure. Experiment and use your judgment as to what sounds best to you.

▶ Watch out for the various accidentals throughout.

BRANLE GAY

Jean Baptiste Besard

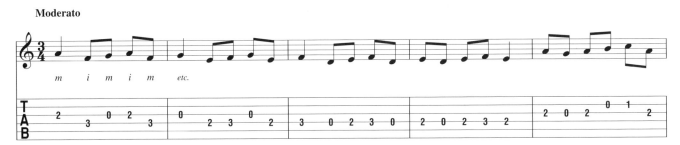

Practice and Performance Tips: Sor

The next piece is from Fernando Sor's *Introduction à l'Étude de la Guitar* ("Introduction to the Study of the Guitar").

▶ The tempo is *allegro* and should be played at about 120 bpm.

▶ Note the right-hand fingering—the *a* is integrated into the pattern. Practice the right-hand fingerings until they are comfortable.

▶ Play this piece with a light, bouncy feel.

OP. 60 NO. 2

Fernando Sor

LESSON #16: REST STROKE

In addition to fingers 1–4, the thumb (*p*) is also used to pluck the strings. Usually, the thumb is assigned to the lower three strings: E (sixth), A (fifth), and D (fourth). Keep in mind, however, that there are exceptions to every rule.

You can pluck notes using *free strokes* or *rest strokes*—regardless of whether you are using your thumb or your other fingers. In this lesson, we'll look at the rest stroke.

How to Play Rest Stroke with the Thumb

Rest strokes are used for notes that require emphasis—in other words, notes that need to be louder or fuller than the others. We'll begin by playing rest strokes with the thumb because the motion should come fairly naturally. To play a rest stroke, do the following:

rest stroke start

1. Position your thumb on the string at a slight angle. The string should be touching the flesh but not quite the thumbnail.

2. Pluck the string in a downward motion with a combination of flesh and thumbnail, coming to rest on the next, adjacent string. When performing the stroke, do not bend the middle two thumb joints. Keep the thumb straight, with the movement originating from the joint where the thumb meets the wrist.

3. Bring the thumb back into position and repeat steps 1 and 2.

Try the preceding steps on the low E (sixth) string, with your thumb coming to rest on the A (fifth) string after each stroke. Strive for a full and pleasing tone.

For our first exercise, we will be playing rest strokes with the thumb on the three lowest strings. We will use simple rhythms at first (in this case, quarter notes) so you can focus on the mechanics of the strokes. Also, as mentioned above, strive for a full and rich tone.

rest stroke follow-through

EXERCISE 1

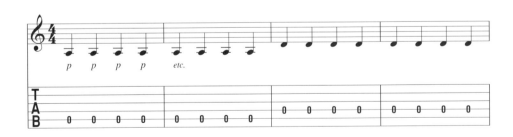

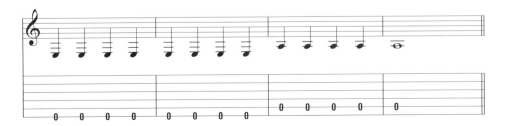

Practice in front of a mirror, if possible, to ensure that you are using proper technique: you should be sitting up straight, your plucking hand should be positioned correctly, and the plucking-hand thumb should remain straight as you pluck. You can set up a small mirror on a tabletop if you do not have a full-length mirror.

For Exercise 2, we'll incorporate the left hand.

EXERCISE 2

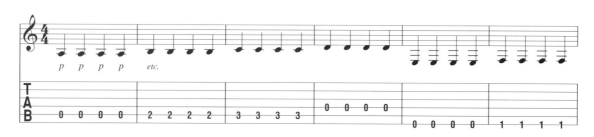

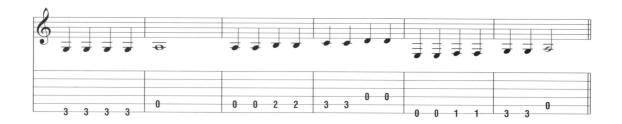

In Exercise 3, we will change notes more rapidly, while also introducing some eighth notes into the rhythm.

EXERCISE 3

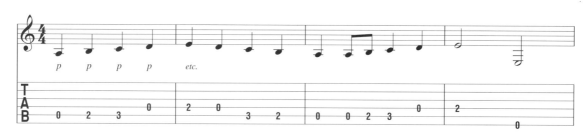

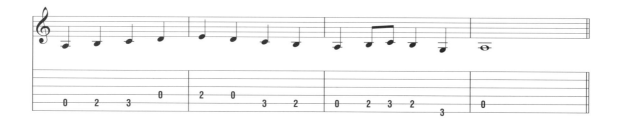

LESSON #17: FREE STROKE

In this lesson, we'll concentrate on playing free stroke with the thumb. This technique is a bit trickier than rest stroke, because you must clear the adjacent string on your follow-through with the thumb. This results in a lighter sound than rest stroke.

How to Play Free Stroke with the Thumb

free stroke start

free stroke follow-through

1. Position your thumb on the string at a slight angle. The string should be touching the flesh but not quite the thumbnail.

2. Pluck the string with a combination of flesh and thumbnail so that it clears the next, adjacent string (this requires a very slight upward motion with the thumb). As with rest stroke, do not bend the middle two thumb joints. Keep the thumb straight, with the movement originating from the joint where the thumb meets the wrist.

3. Bring the thumb back into position and repeat steps 1 and 2.

Try the preceding steps on the low E (sixth) string, clearing the adjacent A (fifth) string after each stroke. Strive for a pleasing tone.

Now let's try some exercises!

Exercise 1 features free strokes with the thumb on the three lowest strings. Focus on the mechanics of the stroke and achieve a clear, well-rounded tone.

EXERCISE 1

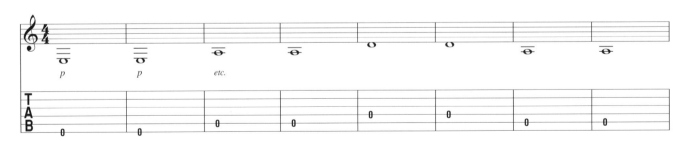

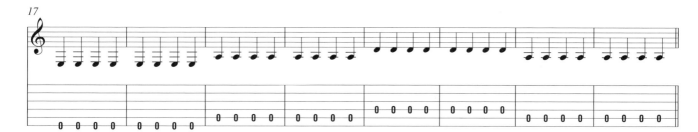

Now let's add some fretted notes while maintaining a simple quarter-note rhythm.

EXERCISE 2

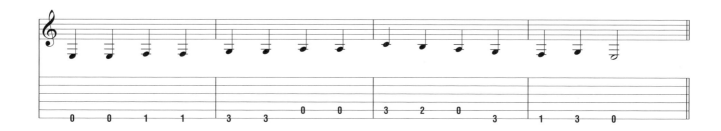

This one really gets your thumb moving. Remember to keep the plucking light and to clear the adjacent strings with each follow-through.

EXERCISE 3

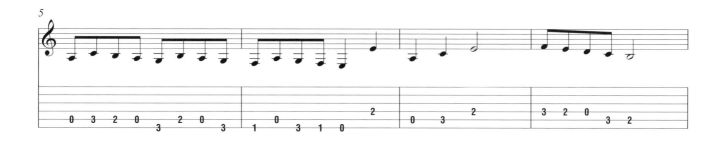

LESSON #18: CHORD TECHNIQUE

In this lesson, we will look at several ways chords can appear in music and the technique for playing them.

The technical definition of a "chord" is three or more notes played simultaneously. Sometimes chords are defined as having two or more notes, but, more accurately, two notes played simultaneously produce a *double stop*. The technique for playing double stops is essential for playing chords, as well, so we will look at those first.

Double Stops

In some cases, double stops are plucked with two fingers, and in other cases, they are plucked with a thumb and a finger. When plucking with more than one finger, use free strokes. When plucking with a thumb and a finger, you also have the option of using rest strokes for the finger. In addition, be sure to first place the fingers on the strings and then pluck inward, toward the palm, without moving the wrist or arm. The pictures below show the starting position and follow-through for each of these types of double stops, using free strokes.

| two fingers start | two fingers follow-through | thumb & finger start | thumb & finger follow-through |

In our first example, we will pluck double stops with two fingers at a time—first with a combination of *i* and *m*, then with *m* and *a*, and finally, with *i* and *a*. Remember to keep your wrist and arm still while your fingers pluck inward, toward the palm.

EXAMPLE 1

In Example 2, you will be plucking with the thumb and either the *m* or *a* finger. Try using all free strokes at first, and then add rest strokes to the downbeats of measures 4, 5, 7, and 8. Notice that upper and lower notes are written as two separate parts, or *voices*. The stems in the upper voice are pointing upward, and the stems in the lower voice are pointing downward. This makes it easy to distinguish between the parts.

EXAMPLE 2

Three-Note Chords

The technique for playing three-note chords is the same as with double stops, and you can play them either by plucking with three fingers or with the thumb and two fingers, depending on what strings are being played. Use free strokes for both of these situations.

In Example 3, we will be plucking with three fingers.

EXAMPLE 3

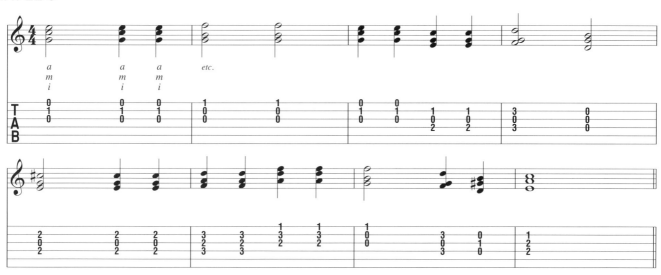

In Example 4, you will be plucking with the thumb and combinations of *m-a*, *i-m*, and *i-a*.

EXAMPLE 4

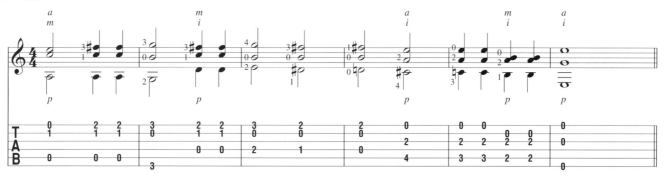

> **A Word About Four-Note Chords** The same techniques apply for four-note chords as with double stops and three-note chords. However, because classical guitar only uses three plucking fingers (*i, m, a*) and the thumb (*p*), that is our only combination of fingers that can be used to form a four-note chord (*p-i-m-a*). Use free strokes for all four-note chords, and remember to pluck inward toward the palm without moving your wrist or arm.

LESSON #19: 2ND–5TH POSITION

The purpose of this lesson is to introduce you to playing in positions 2 through 5. The term *position* refers to a four-fret area where the position of the first finger determines the position name. For instance, in *second position*, the first finger would be located at the second fret, the second finger at the third fret, etc. In *fifth position*, the first finger would be located at the fifth fret, the second finger at the sixth fret, etc. These fingerings will sometimes vary, and on occasion, you will be asked to stretch either a fret higher or lower with the pinky or first finger. Sometimes, though not included here, you may see a Roman numeral above the written music indicating the position.

The reasons for choosing to play in one position rather than another have to do with tone and fingering efficiency, but the focus of this lesson is just to get you reading and playing in these different positions.

Second Position

EXAMPLE 1

EXAMPLE 2

Third Position

EXAMPLE 3

EXAMPLE 4

Fourth Position

EXAMPLE 5

EXAMPLE 6

Fifth Position

EXAMPLE 7

LESSON #20: 6TH-9TH POSITION

Let's familiarize ourselves with reading and playing in positions 6 through 9.

Sixth Position

EXAMPLE 1

EXAMPLE 2

Seventh Position

EXAMPLE 3

EXAMPLE 4

Eighth Position

EXAMPLE 5

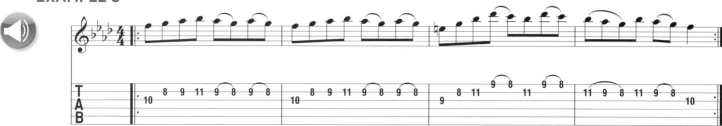

EXAMPLE 6

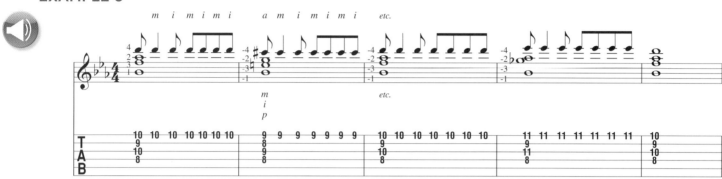

Ninth Position

EXAMPLE 7

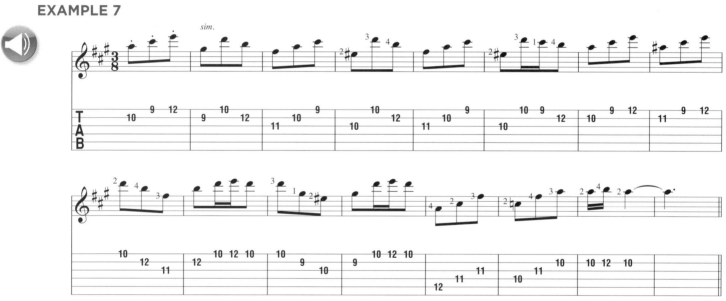

EXAMPLE 8

LESSON #21: MOVABLE SCALES

Movable Scales

The scales in this lesson are *movable*, which means they do not include any open strings. By starting any of these scales on a different tonic (i.e., moving the entire scale form up or down the neck), you will have the same exact scale in a different key. For instance, if you move the first scale below, C major, up two frets to start on the note D, you will have the D major scale.

Vertical Fingerings

In addition, the scales in this lesson are all in one position (with a few stretches here and there). One-position scales are vertical fingerings because they go up and down the scales (and strings) while staying in one position on the neck.

Included in this lesson are four different major-scale fingerings and four different minor-scale fingerings. However, any one of these fingerings can be used to play a major scale in *any* key.

Practice Tips and Right-Hand Fingering

The following are some tips to help you master the scales in this lesson.

▶ Learn one scale at a time, practicing slowly until you are comfortable with the fingering.

▶ Incorporate the new scale into your daily warmup routine.

▶ Memorize the scale. You should be able to play the scale as if it were second nature.

▶ Use a metronome or some other time-keeping device, gradually increasing your tempo.

▶ Always strive for a full, crisp tone across all the notes.

▶ Each time you practice a scale, go through the plucking-hand fingerings below:

- *i–m–i–m–i–m,* etc.
- *im–im–im–im,* etc. (doubling each note)
- *m–a–m–a–m–a,* etc.

- *ma–ma–ma–ma,* etc.
- *i–a–i–a–i–a,* etc.
- *ia–ia–ia–ia,* etc.

C MAJOR SCALE

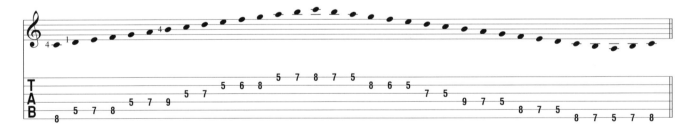

G MAJOR SCALE

D MAJOR SCALE

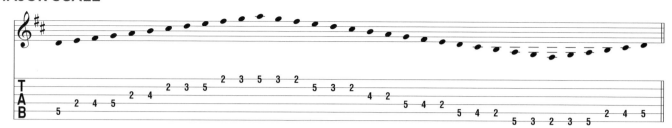

E MAJOR SCALE

A MELODIC MINOR SCALE

E MELODIC MINOR SCALE

B MELODIC MINOR SCALE

C# MELODIC MINOR SCALE

LESSON #22: SCALES WITH POSITION SHIFTS

Horizontal Fingerings

The scales in this chapter feature many position shifts. Because of this, their patterns run horizontally across the fingerboard, as opposed to vertical fingerings that stay in one position.

Included in this lesson are two major-scale fingerings and their relative minors.

Practice Tips

▶ Shifts are indicated in the music by a dash preceding the fretting-hand finger number (–1, –2, etc.). Remember:

- When shifting with the same finger (when the first note of the new position is played with the same finger as the last note of the previous position), release pressure but do not remove the finger from the string, and then move to the new position as cleanly and seamlessly as possible.

- When shifting to a different finger, move into the new position by taking the fingers off the string and repositioning seamlessly with a quick movement of the fretting-hand arm.

- Avoid string noise.

▶ Learn one scale at a time, practicing slowly until you are comfortable with the fingering.

▶ Incorporate the new scale into your daily warmup routine.

▶ Memorize the scale. You should be able to play it with your eyes closed (eventually!).

▶ Use a metronome or some other time-keeping device, gradually increasing your tempo.

▶ Always strive for a full, pleasing tone across all the notes.

▶ Each time you practice a scale, go through the plucking-hand fingerings below:

- *i–m–i–m–i–m*, etc.

- *m–a–m–a–m–a*, etc.

- *i–a–i–a–i–a*, etc.

- *a–m–i, a–m–i, a–m–i, etc.*

C MAJOR SCALE

A MELODIC MINOR SCALE

G MAJOR SCALE

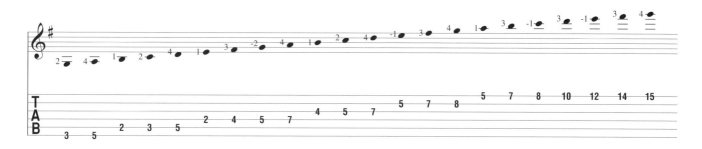

E MELODIC MINOR SCALE

LESSON #23: INTERVALS

Components of an Interval

An *interval* is the distance between two pitches. A *half step* is an example of an interval, as is a *whole step*. Intervals are determined by counting the note names between two pitches, and that gives us a number. For instance, say we are looking for the interval between C and F:

First, we would count the note names in between those two notes, including the notes themselves:

We arrive at the number "4," so our interval is a *4th*.

Intervals also have *qualities*, and there are five types: *major, minor, perfect, augmented,* and *diminished*. For instance, our 4th above is actually a *perfect 4th*. We'll look at the qualities in greater detail later in this lesson.

Intervals of the Major Scale

Intervals of a major scale are determined by the distance between the tonic and the other scale degrees. For example, from the tonic to the second degree of the scale is the interval of a *2nd*, from the tonic to the third degree is a *3rd*, etc. The major scale contains only perfect and major intervals. Below is the C major scale with its intervals labeled.

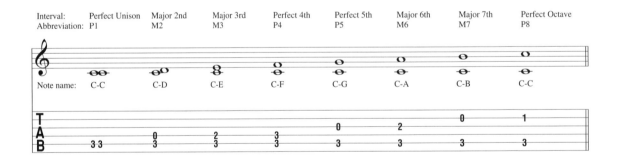

The same formula holds true for every major scale. Check out the intervals of the G major scale below.

More About Interval Qualities

Intervals and interval qualities can be measured in whole steps and half steps. For instance, a minor 2nd is the distance of a half step, while a major 2nd is the distance of a whole step (two half steps).

Half steps determine interval qualities—let's look at how this works:

▶ Lower a major interval by a half step, and you get a minor interval.

▶ Raise a perfect interval by a half step, and you get an augmented interval.

▶ Lower a perfect 5th interval by a half step, and you get a diminished interval.

Intervals Within One Octave

Below are all of the intervals within one octave—in this case, from C to C. The note names and intervals are indicated, as well as abbreviations and distances in whole steps and half steps. Play each interval *harmonically* (at the same time) and *melodically* (one after the other) to get your ears acquainted with the different-sounding intervals. You will notice that some are *consonant* (pleasant sounding), like the major 3rd, and some are *dissonant* (clashing), like the diminished 5th.

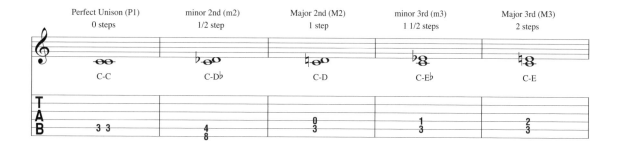

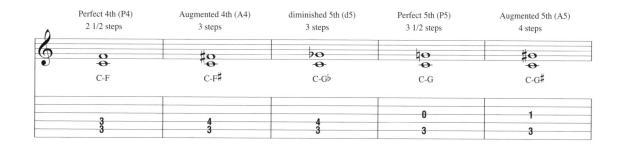

LESSON #24: SCALES IN 3RDS

In this lesson, we'll look at scales harmonized in 3rds. In other words, we'll add an interval of a 3rd on top of each scale tone.

There are two types of 3rds: major 3rds and minor 3rds. An interval of a major 3rd is the distance of two whole steps. A minor 3rd is the distance of a step and a half.

The diagrams below show the fingerings for the major 3rd interval on each string set. Notice that the only aberration from the basic form occurs on strings 2 and 3 because of how the guitar is tuned. (Also, a difference in fingering occurs when open strings are used, which can be seen in the C and G major scales below.)

Major 3rds

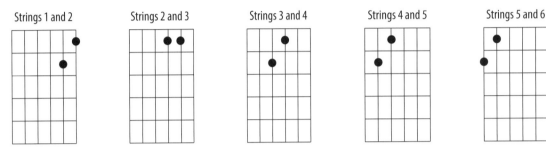

The diagrams below show the fingerings for the minor 3rd interval on each string set. As with the major 3rds, notice that the only aberration from the basic form occurs on strings 2 and 3 because of how the guitar is tuned.

Minor 3rds

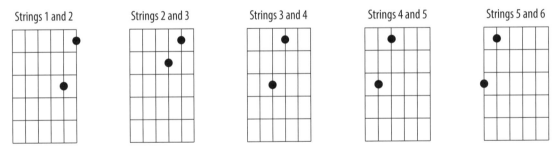

Major Scales

First, let's harmonize major scales in 3rds. When a 3rd is added on top of each scale tone, we get the following pattern, which is the same for every major scale:

Major 3rd–minor 3rd–minor 3rd–Major 3rd–Major 3rd–minor 3rd–minor 3rd–Major 3rd

Let's look at a couple of examples. When practicing these harmonized scales, be sure to release pressure in the fretting-hand fingers—without removing them from the strings—as you climb up and down the neck and reposition for each new interval. Avoid string squeaks and fret buzzes as much as possible, and practice slowly at first. Also, play these scales using a combination of the *i* and *m* fingers, and then *m* and *a*.

C MAJOR HARMONIZED IN 3RDS

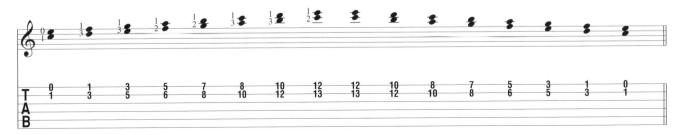

G MAJOR HARMONIZED IN 3RDS

To play any major scale in 3rds, just start with the tonic and apply the aforementioned pattern in 3rds.

Minor Scales

Now let's harmonize minor scales in 3rds. For this purpose, we'll use the harmonic minor scale. When a 3rd is added on top of each scale tone, we get the following pattern, which is the same for every harmonic minor scale:

minor 3rd–minor 3rd–Major 3rd–minor 3rd–Major 3rd–Major 3rd–minor 3rd–minor 3rd

Let's look at a couple of examples. Remember: when practicing these harmonized scales, release pressure in the fretting-hand fingers as you ascend and descend the neck, repositioning for each new interval to produce clear, ringing tones. Again, perform these with right-hand combinations of *i* and *m*, and then *m* and *a*.

D MINOR HARMONIZED IN 3RDS

A MINOR HARMONIZED IN 3RDS

You can play any harmonic minor scale in 3rds by starting with the tonic and applying the aforementioned pattern in 3rds.

LESSON #25: SCALES IN 6THS

Now let's check out scales harmonized in 6ths. Instead of adding an interval of a 6th *above* each scale tone, we will do so *below* each scale tone.

There are two types of 6ths: major 6ths and minor 6ths. An interval of a major 6th is the distance of four-and-a-half steps. A minor 6th is the distance of four steps.

The diagrams below show fingerings for the major 6th interval on each string set. Notice that, because of the guitar's tuning, the fingering shape is identical for the first two string sets, as is the shape for the second two string sets. Notice also that the notes in each shape are two strings apart. (Remember: whenever open strings are introduced, the shape remains the same but the fingering changes, as can be seen in the scales that follow.)

Major 6ths

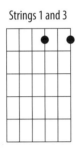
Strings 1 and 3

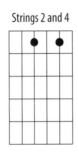
Strings 2 and 4

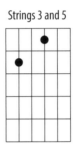
Strings 3 and 5

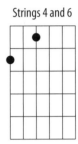
Strings 4 and 6

The diagrams below show the fingerings for the minor 6th interval on each string set. As with the major 6ths, notice that the finger shape is the same for the first two string sets and then for the second two string sets. Compare these diagrams with those above and you will see that we are just lowering the top note by a half step.

Minor 6ths

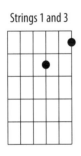
Strings 1 and 3

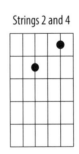
Strings 2 and 4

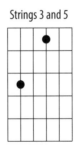
Strings 3 and 5

Strings 4 and 6

Major Scales

First, let's harmonize major scales in 6ths. When a 6th is added below each scale tone, we get the following pattern, which is the same for every major scale:

minor 6th–Major 6th–Major 6th–minor 6th–minor 6th–Major 6th–Major 6th–minor 6th

Let's look at a couple of examples. When practicing these harmonized scales, be sure to release pressure in the fretting-hand fingers—without removing them from the strings—as you climb up and down the neck and reposition for each new interval. Avoid string squeaks and fret buzzes as much as possible, and practice slowly at first. Also, play these scales with a combination of the *p* and *m* fingers.*

C MAJOR HARMONIZED IN 6THS

G MAJOR HARMONIZED IN 6THS

To play any major scale in 6ths, just start with the tonic as the upper note and apply the aforementioned pattern in 6ths.

Minor Scales

Now let's harmonize minor scales in 6ths. For this purpose, we'll use the harmonic minor scale. When a 6th is added below each scale tone, we get the following pattern, which is the same for every harmonic minor scale:

Major 6th–Major 6th–minor 6th–Major 6th–minor 6th–minor 6th–Major 6th–Major 6th

Let's look at a few examples. Remember: when practicing these harmonized scales, release pressure in the fretting-hand fingers as you ascend and descend the neck, repositioning for each new interval to produce clear, ringing tones. Again, perform these with right-hand combinations of *p* and *m* (when using the thumb for the bottom notes, you can also alternate between *i* and *m* for the upper notes), and then *i* and *a*.

E MINOR HARMONIZED IN 6THS

G MINOR HARMONIZED IN 6THS

You can play any harmonic minor scale in 6ths by starting with the tonic as the upper note and applying the aforementioned pattern in 6ths.

*When using the thumb for the bottom notes, you can also alternate between *i* and *m* for the upper notes, and then *i* and *a*.

LESSON #26: SCALES IN 10THS

Let's look at scales harmonized in *10ths*—meaning, we'll add an interval of a 10th above each scale tone. A 10th is an *extended interval*—that is, an interval that spans a distance greater than an octave. In this case, a 10th is the distance of 10 scale tones. For instance, let's say our bottom note is C. Count 10 scale tones from C (**C**–D–E–F–G–A–B–C–D–**E),** and you get E. As you can see, a 10th is the same as a 3rd, just an octave higher.

There are two types of 10ths: major 10ths and minor 10ths. An interval of a major 10th is the distance of eight whole steps. A minor 10th is the distance of seven-and-a-half steps.

The diagrams below show fingerings for the major 10th interval on each string set. Notice that, because of the guitar's tuning, the fingering shape is different for the third string set. Notice also that the notes in each shape have two strings in between them. (Remember: whenever open strings are introduced, the shape remains the same but the fingering changes, as can be seen in the scales that follow.)

Major 10ths

Strings 1 and 4	Strings 2 and 5	Strings 3 and 6
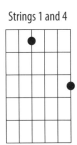	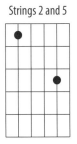	

The diagrams below show the fingerings for the minor 10th interval on each string set. As with the major 10ths, notice that the fingering shape is different for the third string set. Also, compare these diagrams with those above and you will see that we are just lowering the top note by a half step.

Minor 10ths

Strings 1 and 4	Strings 2 and 5	Strings 3 and 6
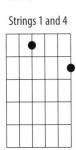		

Major Scales

We'll start by harmonizing major scales in 10ths. When a 10th is added above each scale tone, we get the following pattern, which is the same for every major scale:

Major 10th–minor 10th–minor 10th–Major 10th–Major 10th–minor 10th–minor 10th–Major 10th

Let's look at a couple of examples. When practicing these harmonized scales, be sure to release pressure in the fretting-hand fingers—without removing them from the strings—as you climb up and down the neck, repositioning for each new interval. Avoid string squeaks and fret buzzes as much as possible, and practice slowly at first. Also, play these scales using *p* on the bottom notes and alternating the *i* and *m* fingers on the upper notes.

A MAJOR HARMONIZED IN 10THS

F MAJOR HARMONIZED IN 10THS

To play any major scale in 10ths, just start with the tonic as the lower note and apply the aforementioned pattern in 10ths.

Minor Scales

Now let's harmonize minor scales in 10ths. For this purpose, we'll use the harmonic minor scale. When a 10th is added above each scale tone, we get the following pattern, which is the same for every harmonic minor scale:

minor 10th–minor 10th–Major 10th–minor 10th–Major 10th–Major 10th–minor 10th–minor 10th

Let's look at a few examples. Remember: when practicing these harmonized scales, release pressure in the fretting-hand fingers as you ascend and descend the neck, repositioning for each new interval to produce clear, ringing tones. Again, perform these with *p* on the bottom notes and alternating the *i* and *m* fingers on the upper notes.

D MINOR HARMONIZED IN 10THS

F♯ MINOR HARMONIZED IN 10THS

You can play any harmonic minor scale in 10ths by starting with the tonic as the lower note and applying the aforementioned pattern in 10ths.

A *chord* consists of three or more notes played at the same time. It is important for musicians to understand chords. In this lesson, we'll look at several types of chords and how they are built.

Triads

A *triad* is a three-note chord made up of a *root* (upon which the chord is built and after which the chord is named), 3rd, and 5th. These notes are consecutive 3rds, or every *other* note in a scale, starting with the root. There are four different qualities of triads: *major, minor, augmented,* and *diminished.* We can look at the components of these chords in a couple of ways:

▶ **Intervals from the root:** root–3rd–5th, root–♭3rd–5th, etc.

▶ **Intervals from note to note:** major 3rd–minor 3rd, minor 3rd–major 3rd, etc.

We'll use both of the approaches mentioned above to look at the different types of triads.

Major Triad

A *major triad* is made up of a root, major 3rd, and perfect 5th. From note to note, it contains two intervals: a major 3rd and a minor 3rd.

C MAJOR (C): C–E–G (ROOT–3RD–5TH)

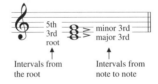

Minor Triad

A *minor triad* is made up of a root, minor 3rd (which can also be referred to as a ♭3rd), and perfect 5th. From note to note, it contains two intervals: a minor 3rd and a major 3rd.

C MINOR (Cm): C–E♭–G (ROOT–♭3RD–5TH)

Augmented Triad

An *augmented triad* is made up of a root, major 3rd, and augmented 5th (which can also be referred to as a ♯5th). From note to note, it contains two intervals: a major 3rd and a major 3rd.

C AUGMENTED (C+): C–E–G♯ (ROOT–3RD–♯5TH)

Diminished Triad

A *diminished triad* is made up of a root, minor 3rd, and diminished 5th (also known as a ♭5th). From note to note, it contains two intervals: a minor 3rd and a minor 3rd.

C DIMINISHED (C°): C–E♭–G♭ (ROOT–♭3RD–♭5TH)

Seventh Chords

A *seventh chord* is a four-note chord and is also made up of consecutive 3rds. It consists of a root, 3rd, 5th, and 7th. There are five common qualities of seventh chord: *major seventh, minor seventh, dominant seventh, minor seventh flat-five (half-diminished seventh),* and *diminished seventh.*

Major Seventh

A *major seventh* chord is made up of a root, major 3rd, perfect 5th, and major 7th. From note to note, it contains three intervals: a major 3rd, a minor 3rd, and a major 3rd. This can also be thought of as a major triad with a major 7th on top.

C MAJOR SEVENTH (Cmaj7): C–E–G–B (ROOT–3RD–5TH–7TH)

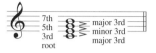

Minor Seventh

A *minor seventh* chord is made up of a root, minor 3rd, perfect 5th, and minor 7th (♭7th). From note to note, it contains three intervals: a minor 3rd, a major 3rd, and a minor 3rd. This can also be thought of as a minor triad with a minor 7th on top.

C MINOR SEVENTH (Cm7): C–E♭–G–B♭ (ROOT–♭3RD–5TH–♭7TH)

Dominant Seventh

A *dominant seventh* chord is made up of a root, major 3rd, perfect 5th, and minor 7th. From note to note, it contains three intervals: a major 3rd, a minor 3rd, and a minor 3rd. This can also be thought of as a major triad with a minor 7th on top.

C DOMINANT SEVENTH (C7): C–E–G–B♭ (ROOT–3RD–5TH–♭7TH)

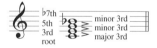

Minor Seventh Flat-Five (Half-Diminished Seventh)

A *minor seventh flat-five* chord is made up of a root, minor 3rd, diminished 5th, and minor 7th. From note to note, it contains three intervals: a minor 3rd, a minor 3rd, and a major 3rd. This can also be thought of as a diminished triad with a minor 7th on top.

C MINOR SEVENTH FLAT-FIVE (Cm7♭5): C–E♭–G♭–B♭ (ROOT–♭3RD–♭5TH–♭7TH)

Diminished Seventh

A *diminished seventh* chord is made up of a root, minor 3rd, diminished 5th, and diminished 7th (♭♭7th). From note to note, it contains three intervals: a minor 3rd, a minor 3rd, and a minor 3rd. This can also be thought of as a diminished triad with a diminished 7th on top.

C DIMINISHED SEVENTH (C°7): C–E♭–G♭–B♭♭ (ROOT–♭3RD–♭5TH–♭♭7TH)

LESSON #28: MAJOR DIATONIC HARMONY

Harmony is created when notes are sounded simultaneously to produce chords. The term *diatonic* means "belonging to the key." So, *major diatonic harmony* refers to all the chords that belong to a particular major key. We'll look at how this system works—first, with triads, and then with seventh chords.

Triads

To find the diatonic harmony belonging to any key, we need to *stack 3rds* on top of each scale tone. (To "stack 3rds" means to add every *other* note from the scale.) If we stack two 3rds on top of each scale tone, we have a series of triads, or three-note chords. We'll start with the C major scale. Because there are seven scale tones, there are seven different chords in the key of C major:

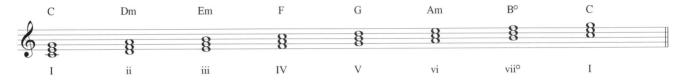

The order of chords in every major key is always the same: **major–minor–minor–major–major–minor–diminished**. As can be seen above, Roman numerals indicate a chord's position in a given key. Uppercase Romans indicate major chords, lowercase Romans are used for minor chords, and lowercase Romans followed by a degree symbol ° are used for diminished chords. So, if you were to mention the ii chord ("two chord") in the key of C, you would be talking about Dm. If you mentioned the vi chord ("six chord") in the key of C, you would be talking about Am.

Roman Numeral Review

I, i = 1

II, ii = 2

III, iii = 3

IV, iv = 4

V, v = 5

VI, vi = 6

VII, vii = 7

More Examples

Let's look at a couple of other examples. Below is a harmonized A major scale. Notice that the chord qualities and Roman numerals are exactly the same as in the key of C.

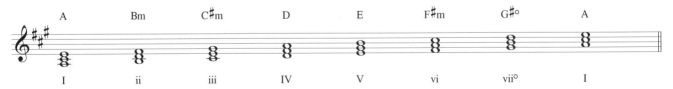

Here's one more example, this time in the key of E major:

As you can see by now, the diatonic triads of a major key can be broken down as follows:

Major	I, IV, V
Minor	ii, iii, vi
Diminished	vii°

Seventh Chords

When we stack one more 3rd on top of each scale tone, we get a series of seventh chords that belong to the key. Here is the C major scale harmonized in seventh chords:

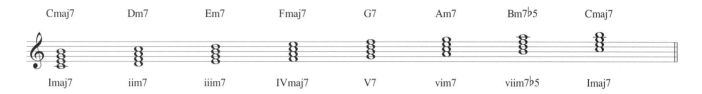

The order of seventh chords in every major key is always the same: **major seventh–minor seventh–minor seventh–major seventh–dominant seventh–minor seventh–half-diminished seventh**. Note that the half-diminished seventh chord is also referred to as a minor seventh flat-five chord.

Here are two more examples of major scales harmonized in seventh chords—first, in A major, and then in E major.

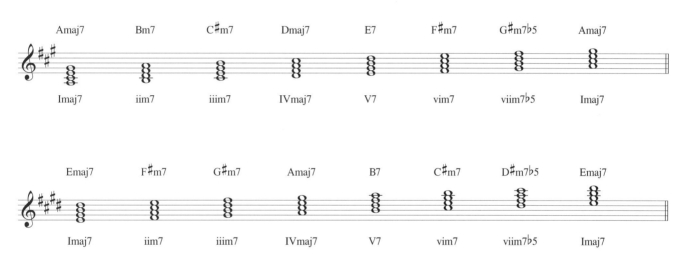

As can be seen above, the diatonic seventh chords of a major key can be broken down like this:

Major Seventh	Imaj7, IVmaj7
Minor Seventh	iim7, iiim7, vim7
Dominant Seventh	V7
Half-Diminished Seventh	viim7♭5

NATURAL MINOR DIATONIC HARMONY

Introduction to Minor Diatonic Harmony

There are three types of minor scales, and so there are three different sets of minor diatonic chords (the chords that belong to a minor key). Minor diatonic harmony borrows from all three of the harmonized scales, so it is important to familiarize yourself with all three. Here, we will look at the diatonic triads and seventh chords for the natural minor scales. To harmonize a scale, we stack consecutive 3rds on top of each scale tone.

The diatonic chords for the natural minor scale are the same as the relative major scale. The Roman numerals, however, are reassigned to start with the tonic of the scale—in other words, the vi chord in a major key becomes the i chord of the minor key.

Triads

Below is the A natural minor scale harmonized in triads.

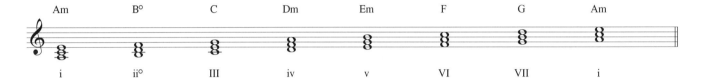

The order of triads for every harmonized natural minor scale is always the same:

minor–diminished–major–minor–minor–major–major

Here are two more examples of natural minor scales harmonized in triads—first, in E minor, and then in B minor. Note that the chord qualities and Roman numerals are exactly the same, regardless of the key.

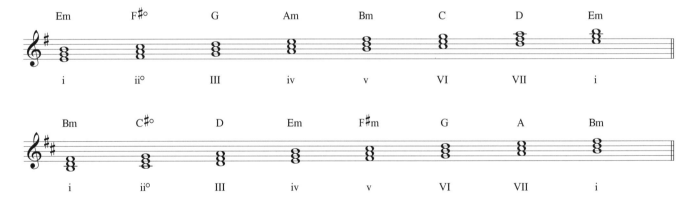

As you can see from the examples above, the diatonic triads of the natural minor scale can be broken down in the following way.

Minor	i, iv, v
Major	III, VI, VII
Diminished	ii°

Seventh Chords

Let's stack one more 3rd on top of the triads to give us the seventh chords for the harmonized natural minor scale.

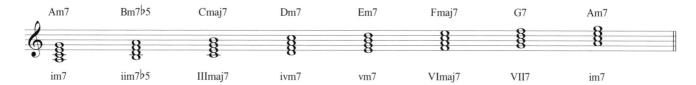

The order of seventh chords in every harmonized natural minor scale is always the same:

minor seventh–half-diminished seventh–major seventh–minor seventh–minor seventh–major seventh–dominant seventh

Below are two more examples of natural minor scales harmonized in seventh chords—first, in E minor, and then in B minor. Remember: the chord qualities and Roman numerals are exactly the same for all natural minor scales harmonized in seventh chords, regardless of key.

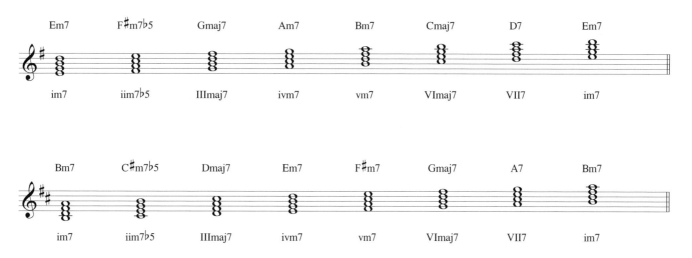

Following is the breakdown for the seventh chords of the natural minor scale:

Minor Seventh	im7, ivm7, vm7
Major Seventh	IIImaj7, VImaj7
Dominant Seventh	VII7
Half-Diminished Seventh	iim7♭5

LESSON #30: HARMONIC MINOR DIATONIC HARMONY

Compared to the natural minor scale, the harmonic minor scale has a raised 7th.

Triads

When the harmonic minor scale is harmonized in triads, the raised 7th produces two diminished chords (the ii° and vii°), an augmented chord (III+), and very importantly, a major V chord, which, along with the V7 chord (covered later in this lesson), is the most common type of V chord used.

We'll look first at the A harmonic minor scale harmonized in triads.

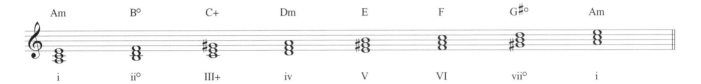

The order of triads for every harmonized harmonic minor scale is always the same:

minor–diminished–augmented–minor–major–major–diminished

Below, we will look at two more examples of harmonic minor scales harmonized in triads—first, in E minor, and then in B minor. Remember: the chord qualities and Roman numerals will always be the same, regardless of key.

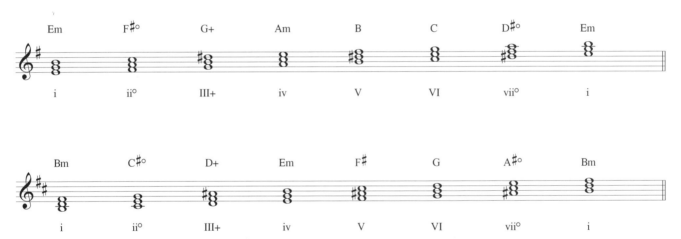

Here is how the harmonic minor triads break down:

Minor	i, iv
Major	V, VI
Diminished	ii°, vii°
Augmented	III+

Seventh Chords

When we stack one more 3rd on top of our triads, we get the diatonic seventh chords of the harmonic minor scale. This produces a *minor/major seventh* chord, im(maj7), which is a minor triad with a major 7th on top. It also creates an *augmented major seventh*, IIImaj7#5, which is an augmented triad with a major 7th on top. Additionally, we get a fully diminished seventh for our vii chord (vii°7) and a dominant seventh for our V chord (V7).

The following is the A harmonic minor scale harmonized in seventh chords.

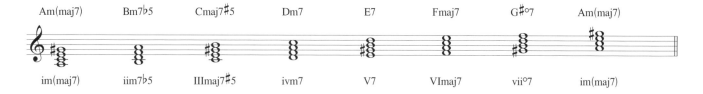

The order of seventh chords in every harmonized harmonic minor scale is always the same:

minor/major seventh–half-diminished seventh–augmented major seventh–minor seventh–dominant seventh–major seventh–diminished seventh

Below are two more examples of harmonic minor scales harmonized in seventh chords—first, in E minor, and then in B minor.

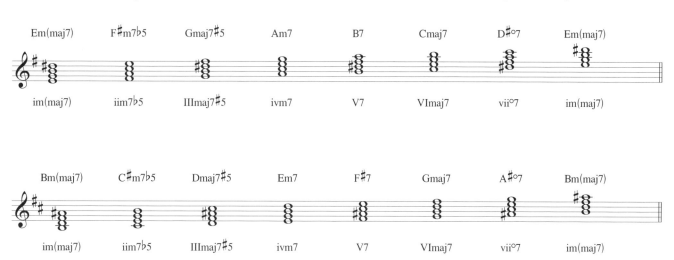

Following is the breakdown for the seventh chords of the harmonic minor scale. As you can see, when the harmonic minor scale is harmonized in seventh chords, it produces a different type of chord on each scale tone.

Minor/major Seventh	im(maj7)
Half-Diminished Seventh	iim7♭5
Augmented Major Seventh	IIImaj7#5
Minor Seventh	ivm7
Dominant Seventh	V7
Major Seventh	VImaj7
Diminished Seventh	vii°7

LESSON #31: MELODIC MINOR DIATONIC HARMONY

Compared to the natural minor scale, the melodic minor scale has raised sixth and seventh tones when ascending.

Triads

When the melodic minor scale is harmonized in triads, the raised 6th and 7th produce two consecutive minor chords (i and ii), two consecutive major chords (IV and V), two consecutive diminished chords (vi° and vii°), and an augmented chord (III+).

Let's look first at the A melodic minor scale harmonized in triads.

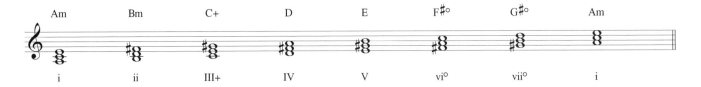

The order of triads for every harmonized melodic minor scale is always the same:

minor–minor–augmented–major–major–diminished–diminished

Below, we will look at two more examples of melodic minor scales harmonized in triads—first, in E minor, and then in B minor. Remember: the chord qualities and Roman numerals will always be the same, regardless of key.

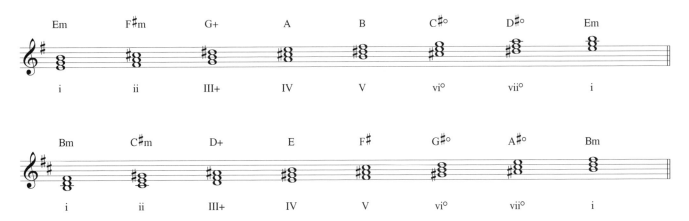

Here is a breakdown of the melodic minor triads:

Minor	i, ii
Augmented	III+
Major	IV, V
Diminished	vi°, vii°

Seventh Chords

When we stack one more 3rd on top of our triads, we get the diatonic seventh chords of the melodic minor scale. This produces a minor/major seventh chord, im(maj7), a minor seventh, iim7, and an augmented major seventh, IIImaj7♯5. Additionally, we get two consecutive dominant seventh chords (IV7 and V7) and two consecutive half-diminished seventh chords (vim7♭5 and viim7♭5).

The following is the A melodic minor scale harmonized in seventh chords.

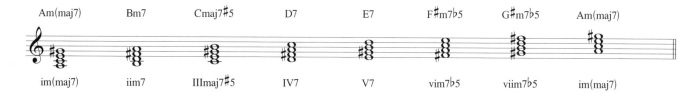

The order of seventh chords in every harmonized melodic minor scale is always the following:

minor/major seventh–minor seventh–augmented major seventh–dominant seventh–dominant seventh–half-diminished seventh–half-diminished seventh

Below are two more examples of melodic minor scales harmonized in seventh chords—first, in E minor, and then in B minor.

The following is a breakdown of the seventh chords of the melodic minor scale. The consecutive sets of dominant seventh and half-diminished seventh chords give this harmonic system a unique sound.

Minor/Major Seventh	im(maj7)
Minor Seventh	iim7
Augmented Major Seventh	IIImaj7♯5
Dominant Seventh	IV7, V7
Half-Diminished Seventh	vim7♭5, viim7♭5

LESSON #32: ADDING BASS NOTES TO MELODIES, PART 1

Now we'll start adding bass notes to melodies. This is the point at which our examples really start to sound "classical." The melody and bass line are considered two different parts, or *voices*. Check out Example 1 below. You'll see that the stems in the upper voice are pointing upward, while the stems in the lower voice are pointing downward. This makes it easy to distinguish between the parts. Typically, the lower voice is plucked by the thumb (*p*), and the upper voice is plucked by a combination of *i*, *m*, and *a*. Keep in mind that when playing more than one part, the fingers of the plucking hand may not alternate strictly. In addition, the fretting-hand fingers may also veer away from strict position fingering to facilitate smooth and efficient movement between notes.

When playing bass notes and melody, make sure your thumb is pointing toward your fretting hand. When you look down, you should see a "V" formed between the thumb and the other plucking-hand fingers.

Open Notes in the Bass

Example 1 features a quarter-note melody in the upper voice and long open notes in the bass. With open-string notes in the bass, you don't have to worry about fretting the melody and bass simultaneously—which makes this a great first example. Play all of the notes using free stroke. Also, to get a feel for the voices, practice them separately at first, and then combine them.

EXAMPLE 1

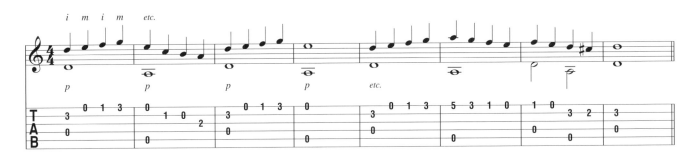

Fretted Notes in the Bass

When bass notes are fretted, things become more challenging. You must keep the bass note planted and ringing for its full value while the upper voice moves above it. This approach is featured in Example 2. Practice each measure separately and then put all the pieces together. The downbeat of measure 1 presents another technical challenge: the F and A notes are on adjacent strings, so both the thumb and *m* finger need to pluck their respective note without cutting off the note on the other string. This is achieved by executing extremely clean free strokes. If it is not working for you, lift the fingers from the strings as soon as you can after plucking them. Practice the motion slowly until you get it.

EXAMPLE 2

Bass Notes by Themselves

Bass notes do not need to be played simultaneously with melody notes—they can be played on any beat by themselves. For instance, in Example 3, the majority of the bass notes are played alone on the downbeat of each measure. Of course, the bass notes ring out while the melody notes follow. Additionally, for ease of reading, sometimes the music will be written in only one voice, like the last measure.

EXAMPLE 3: EXCERPT FROM *OP. 60, NO. 5* IN A MINOR BY FERNANDO SOR

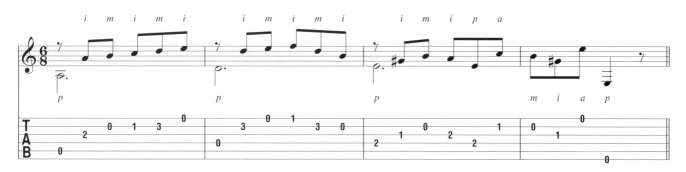

Movement in the Bass

The bass line can also feature the majority of the movement, with longer, sustained notes in the upper voice.

EXAMPLE 4: EXCERPT FROM "MAESTOSO" BY MAURO GIULIANI

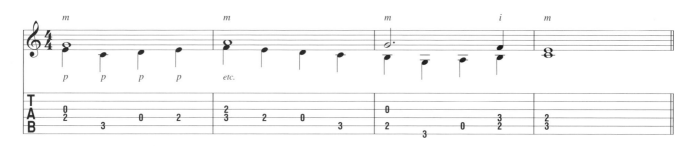

Contrary Motion

Contrary motion is when two simultaneous voices are moving in opposite directions. For instance, in the next example, the upper voice is ascending, and the lower voice is descending.

EXAMPLE 5

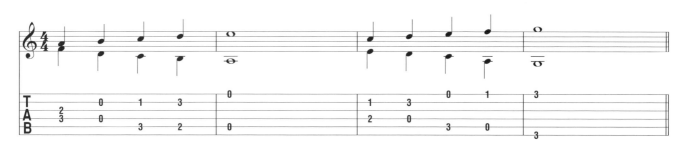

This lesson features bass notes combined with melodies in the context of real pieces.

Practice and Performance Tips: Giuliani

The first piece we'll look at is "Maestoso" by Mauro Giuliani, which is a great example of movement in the bass alternating with movement in the upper voice. There are also instances of contrary motion, as in measure 9.

▶ The title of this piece is a directive for how it is supposed to be played—*maestoso* is Italian for "majestic," "stately," and "dignified."

▶ The tempo is *moderato*, or around 120 bpm. Remember: the tempo should not be rigid at the expense of musicality. You don't want to sound like a robot!

▶ Be sure to follow the fretting-hand indications, as they will help you with some tricky transitions.

▶ Because there is a lot of movement in the bass, pluck lightly and freely with your thumb.

▶ While the thumb should be played entirely with free strokes, try using rest strokes in the upper voice on the downbeats of measures 5, 7, and 9.

MAESTOSO

Mauro Giuliani

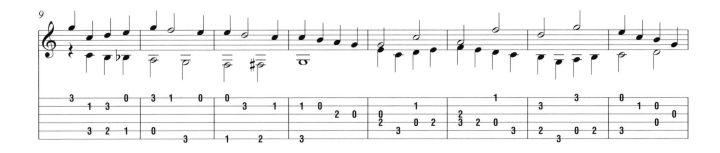

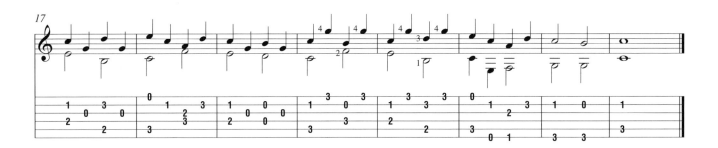

Practice and Performance Tips: Bach

Next is a bourrée from J. S. Bach's *Violin Partita No. 1 in B minor*. A bourrée is an old, hearty French dance used in the Baroque period.

▶ The tempo here is *moderato*. Like the previous piece, play this one at about 120 bpm.

▶ The majority of movement is in the upper voice (with some contrary motion in measures 3 and 23). However, measures 15–16 call for the thumb to play consecutive melody notes on the fourth string. Do not lean on these notes too heavily, as they need to match the tone and volume of the other notes played by the *m* finger in those measures.

▶ Watch out for the left-hand stretches in measures 8 and 12. You can use artistic license to slow down just a bit in order to switch from the fourth finger to the first.

▶ Try using rest strokes to emphasize the downbeat of measure 11 and the third beat of measure 17. Also, watch for the adjacent strings in measures 5, 8, 9, and 10.

BOURRÉE
(FROM *VIOLIN PARTITA NO. 1 IN B MINOR*)

J. S. Bach

LESSON #34: ALTERNATING CHORD FRAGMENTS

Another title for this lesson could be "Alternating Double Stops with Single Notes." However, the double stops and single notes in this lesson combine to make chords. The technique for playing these alternating chord fragments is the same as playing chords: pluck the notes inward, toward the palm, without moving your wrist or arm. The only difference is that the double stops and single notes are played separately rather than simultaneously, as with chords. Let's look at an example.

In the example below, the double stop is plucked with *p* and *m*, and the single note is plucked with *i* (though there are other combinations that you will encounter). In this example, the chord fragments—double-stop C and E and single-note G—make up the C chord.

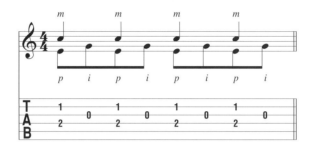

Next, we will learn a piece consisting almost entirely of alternating chord fragments.

"Andantino": Overview and Performance Notes

"Andantino" has two distinct sections, which we can refer to as "A" and "B." The form of the piece is AABABA. In the A sections, the double stops are played by either *p* and *m* or *p* and *a*, and the single notes are played by *i*. In the B sections, the double stops are played by *i* and *m*, and the single notes are played by *p*. Remember to execute the chord technique mentioned above as cleanly and evenly as possible. As the title implies, this piece should be played a little faster than a walking pace—in this case, 80 bpm.

ANDANTINO

Matteo Carcassi

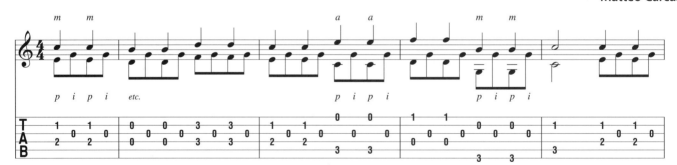

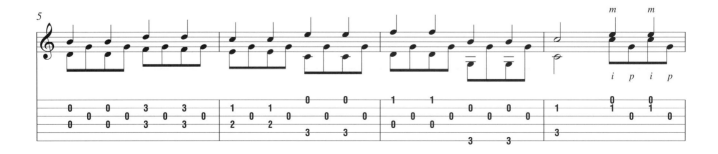

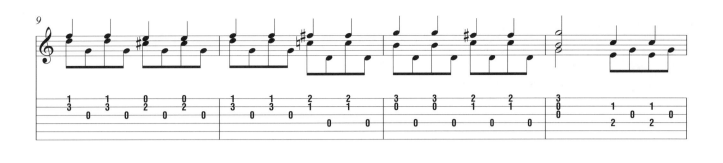

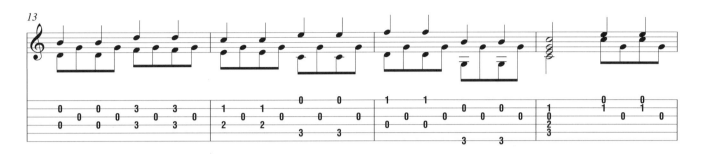

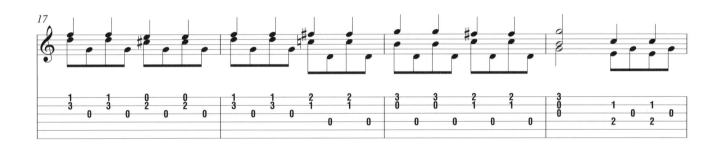

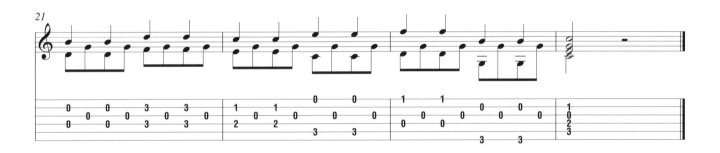

LESSON #35: ADDING CHORDS TO MELODIES

Chords are sometimes used as accompaniment to melodies, creating a full, rich sound. Similar to playing melodies with bass-note accompaniments, your plucking-hand thumb should point toward your fretting hand so that when you look down, a "V" is formed between the thumb and the other plucking-hand fingers.

Below, we will look at a few different ways in which chords can be used to accompany a melody line.

Melody on Top

Our first example features a familiar melody played on top of a chord accompaniment. Practice it slowly at first and make sure each chord rings out for its full value underneath the melody line. This will require you to hold certain notes of the chord with your fretting hand while also playing melody notes with the same hand.

EXAMPLE 1: "ODE TO JOY" FROM BEETHOVEN'S SYMPHONY NO. 9

*See "Rolled Chords" below.

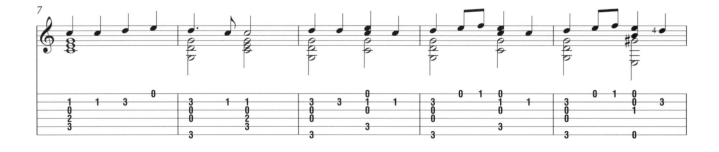

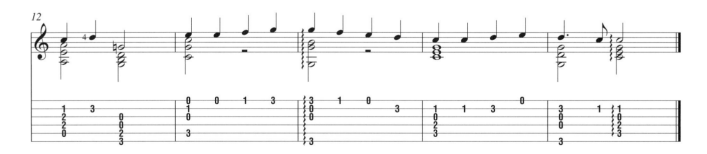

ROLLED CHORDS

In the example above, notice the wavy vertical lines next to the chords in measures 2, 6, 14, and 16. This symbol indicates a rolled chord, or *quasi arpi* ("harp-like"). When you see this symbol, do not pluck all the chord tones simultaneously; instead, play, or "roll," them in quick succession to produce a harp-like effect. Feel free to try this technique on various chords, but don't overdo it—too much of a good thing will detract from its impact, in addition to making the piece sound monotonous!

Melody in the Bass

The melody can also be found in the bass, with chordal accompaniment above. It is relatively easy to bring out a bass melody, as the thumb naturally plucks with more weight than the other fingers and the lower strings are thicker and louder than the upper strings. Check out the following example:

EXAMPLE 2

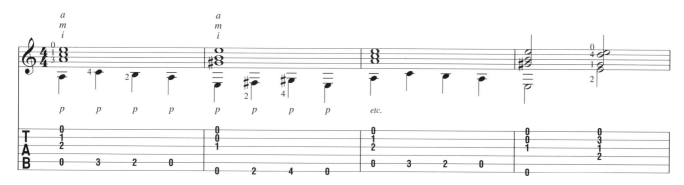

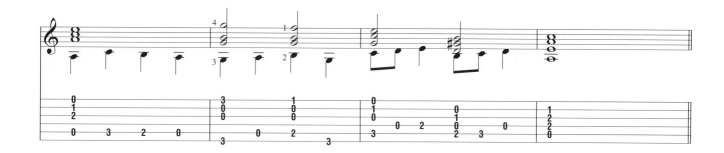

Melody in the Middle

Next, we have a trickier situation: melody in the middle voice. In the example below, notice there is an upper, lower, and middle voice. Be sure to bring out the middle line and let the other two voices serve as accompaniment. This will take some practice, but it is well worth the effort as it produces a unique sound. In addition, follow the left-hand fingerings to ensure smooth transitions from chord to chord.

EXAMPLE 3

LESSON #36: PEDAL POINT

Pedal point (which can also be referred to as *pedal note*, *pedal tone*, or just *pedal*) is a sustained or continually repeated note, usually in the bass, above which other voices move. The term "pedal" was derived from the low notes on a keyboard that could be held indefinitely using foot pedals.

Pedal point can create tension in music, especially if chords are changing above it. In these instances, pedal tones may even act as suspensions calling out for resolution.

There are several types of pedal point, and the first we will look at is the most common.

Standard Pedal Point

In *standard pedal point*, the pedal tones are in the bass. In Example 1, the note A is the pedal tone, and the upper voice progresses through a series of chords.

EXAMPLE 1

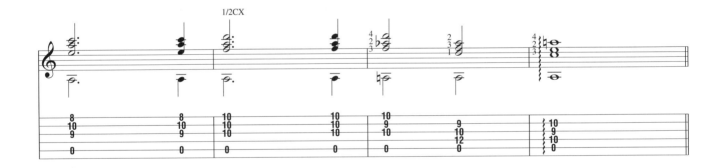

This next example features arpeggios in the upper voice over a D pedal tone.

EXAMPLE 2

Example 3 has an E pedal tone under a single-note melody in the upper voice.

EXAMPLE 3

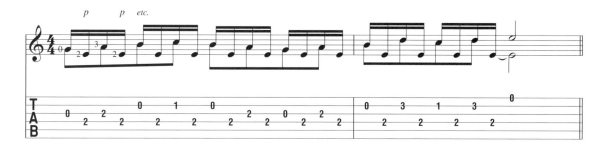

Inverted Pedal Point

When the pedal tone is in the upper voice, the result is an *inverted pedal point*. Our pedal tone in Example 4 is the D note played on the second string.

EXAMPLE 4

Internal Pedal Point

Internal pedal point is when the pedal tone is in the middle voice. Below, the upper voice is ascending, the voice in the bass is descending, and the pedal tone remains an A in between those two voices.

EXAMPLE 5

Pedal-Point Phrases

The last type of pedal we'll look at is a *pedal-point phrase*. Here, our pedal is not just a single note, but a couple of notes or even a phrase. In Example 6, our lower voice runs through a series of chords while the upper voice pedals the phrase: E–G–E–G–E–G–E.

EXAMPLE 6

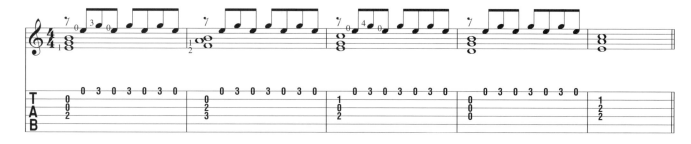

LESSON #37: STUDY NO. 1, OP. 60 (CARCASSI)

Overview

Matteo Carcassi's *25 Studies, Op. 60* is a staple of classical guitar study and repertoire. "Study No. 1" is a scale-oriented piece with several chord-based sections (for instance, measures 29–36). This study is a workout for both the fretting and plucking hands and features a steady stream of eighth notes. Because there is little rhythmic variation, it is important to make the piece as musical as possible. Some suggestions for this are listed below.

Performance and Practice Notes

▶ The tempo for "Study No. 1" is *allegro* and should be played at about 130 bpm.

▶ The repetitive eighth-note rhythm of this piece may get monotonous if played exactly to tempo all the way through. Therefore, play this piece *rubato*, or with a flexible tempo, slowing down and speeding up according to what sounds good to you.

▶ There are several position changes to watch out for—for example, in measures 9–10, 29–34, and 38–39. Be sure to execute these transitions as cleanly and smoothly as possible, and avoid making squeaking sounds on the strings with your fingers when shifting.

▶ Another way to give this piece some expression is to use dynamics. Follow the dynamics indicated in the music, but experiment with your own, as well.

STUDY NO. 1, OP. 60

Matteo Carcassi

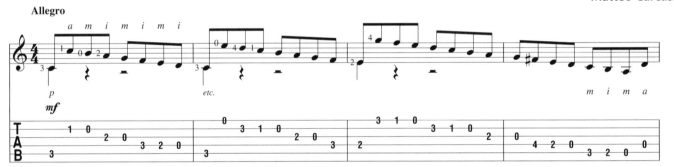

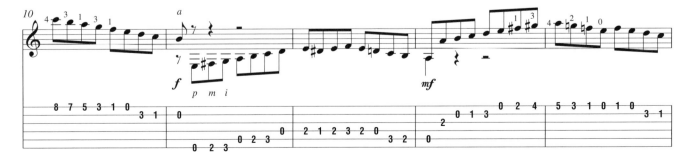

STUDY NO. 2, OP. 60 (CARCASSI)

Overview

"Study No. 2," from Carcassi's *25 Studies, Op. 60,* is similar to the first study in that it features the same rhythm throughout—in this case, a steady stream of 16th notes. Because of this, it is necessary to play this piece with expression and a tempo infused with personal interpretation. Unlike the first study, "Study No. 2" is a chord-oriented piece.

Performance and Practice Notes

▶ The tempo is *andante* and should be played at about 80 bpm.

▶ At first, it may be a challenge to maintain the steady 16th-note pulse with the plucking hand. Practice the finger pattern (*p–i–m–a, m–i–a–m*) over and over, using just one chord with the fretting hand—for instance, the first two beats of the first measure. This will in effect "automate" the plucking hand so you can then concentrate on the fretting-hand movements.

▶ There are many position changes throughout this piece. Be sure to execute these transitions seamlessly. An extreme example of this is the shift from 10th position to first position when moving from measure 20 to measure 21. Practice this shift over and over until it's perfect.

▶ Play this piece with a *rubato* feel. Also, once you have the mechanics down, use the dynamic markings as a springboard for your own expressive interpretation.

STUDY NO. 2, OP. 60

Matteo Carcassi

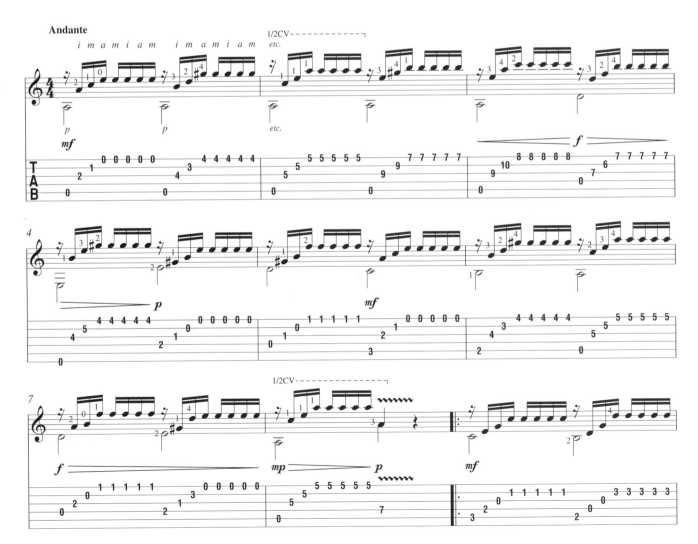

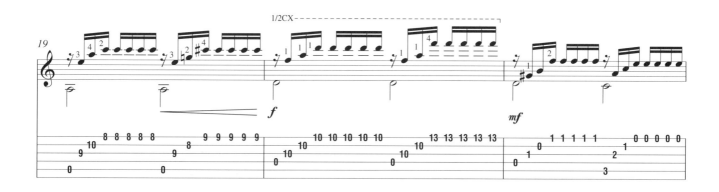

LESSON #39: STUDY NO. 7, OP. 60 (CARCASSI)

Overview

Like "Study No. 2" from Carcassi's *25 Studies, Op. 60,* "Study No. 7" also features a steady stream of 16th notes. The melody is in the bass throughout and many sections feature a pedal tone in the upper voice—for instance, the repetitive A note in measure 1. This is a dramatic piece that benefits from a good sense of dynamics and strong, confident technique.

Performance and Practice Notes

▶ The tempo is *allegro* and should be played at about 120 bpm. It will require practice to get this piece up to speed. Start as slowly as you need in order to play clear and steady 16th notes, then gradually increase the speed.

▶ "Study No. 7" is another great plucking-hand workout. The pattern *p–a–m–i, p–a–m–i* is indicated for much of the piece; practice this over and over until it is comfortable. You can play the first measure repeatedly, without stopping, until you get the hang of the plucking-hand fingering.

▶ As mentioned in the overview above, the melody is in the bass, so make sure that all the bass notes ring out clearly and for their full value. A couple of places require you to mute the bass note; for example, in measure 8, you want the A to ring for only two beats.

▶ It is important to follow the fretting-hand fingerings, as many of the transitions would be awkward if fingered differently. However, feel free to experiment with your own ideas.

▶ Finally, try using rest strokes on the first notes of selected slurs, like the F note on beat 2 of measure 8.

STUDY NO. 7, OP. 60

Matteo Carcassi

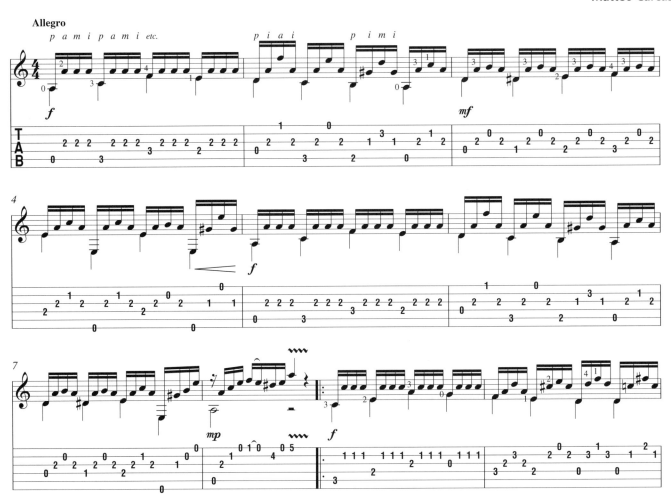

LESSON #40: BARRE CHORDS

When you press a single finger across more than one string at the same fret, you are forming a *barre*. Many chords utilize this technique.

A *full barre* (or *great barre*) occurs when you place a single finger across all six strings. A *half barre* (or *small barre*) occurs when you place a single finger across two to five strings. Barre chords are movable, which means you can move them up and down the fingerboard and they will maintain their quality (major, minor, etc.), but their letter names will change (Gm at the third fret would become Am at the fifth fret, and so on).

It takes more strength to play a full barre than a half barre, but the basic technique is the same, and you should remember the following for both:

▸ Keep your fretting-hand elbow at your side. Drop, or "curve," your wrist to accommodate the lower strings and provide strength for the barre (see Photo 1).

▸ Do not retain tension in your fingers, but allow the weight of your arm and wrist to provide the necessary gripping strength. Do not grip too hard—use only the strength necessary to execute the barre.

▸ Though your fingers are laying flat across the strings, you don't have to apply pressure to all the notes at the same time. Figure out which notes in the chord need to ring out and apply pressure at the appropriate part (or parts) of the finger to produce those tones (see Photo 2).

The Half Barre

Remember: for a half barre, you are laying a finger across two to five strings. In written music, a half barre is indicated with "1/2C" ("C" stands for "capo," Italian for "beginning"; you may also see "B" used for "barre"), followed by the Roman numeral of the position in which the barre occurs. To make the notation more specific, the fraction is often adjusted to reflect the exact number of barred strings. For example, if your first finger were placed across the top three strings at the third fret, you would see "1/2C III" above the chord. If your first finger were placed across the top five strings at the third fret, you would see "5/6C III," indicating that five out of six strings are barred. The fractions are usually distilled down to the lowest common denominator as well, so if you were barring only two strings, then you would see "1/3," instead of "2/6."

The following are photos showing examples of half barres. (**Note:** When barring with your first finger, place it just slightly on its side, toward the thumb.)

1: Keep fretting-hand elbow at your side. Drop, or "curve," your wrist to accommodate the lower strings and provide strength for the barre.

2: Only apply pressure where needed. For instance, in this photo, we only want the notes on the first, second, and sixth strings to ring out. So, we do not need to apply pressure to the middle strings with the middle joint of our first finger; instead, press only with the base and tip of the finger. This is an efficient use of strength and will allow you to play for longer without your wrist and fingers getting tired.

G chord (1/2C III)   D chord (5/6C V)

Dm chord (1/2C X)

Below is an example that features half-barre chords.

EXAMPLE 1

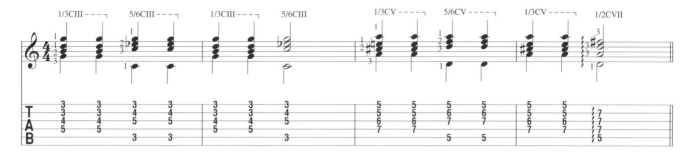

The Full Barre

As mentioned, for a full barre, you are laying a finger across all six strings. A full barre is indicated with "C," followed by the Roman numeral of the position in which the barre occurs. So, if your first finger were placed across all six strings at the seventh fret, you would see "C VII" above the chord. Here are photos showing examples of full barres:

A chord (C V)   Fm chord (C I)   C7 chord (C VIII)

Now let's play an example featuring the full barre.

EXAMPLE 2

LESSON #41: "MINUETTO SCHERZANDO" (SCARLATTI)

Overview

Alessandro Scarlatti (1660–1725) was a Baroque composer famous for his operas. Considered the founder of the *Neapolitan School* (a group of composers who worked in Naples, Italy), Scarlatti's music exhibited a sense of poetry and drama, which is evident in "Minuetto Scherzando."

Minuetto is Italian for "minuet," and *scherzando* means "lively" or "playful." This lively minuet comprises three parts, the first two of which are repeated. The last section is a variation of the first.

Performance and Practice Notes

FRETTING-HAND MUTING

This piece presents a bit of a technical challenge with respect to making sure that notes last only for their written value. Of course, there is room for interpretation, but an attempt should be made to stay true to the composer's vision. The issue arises mainly in the bass line. Look at measures 1 and 2 below.

MEASURES 1–2

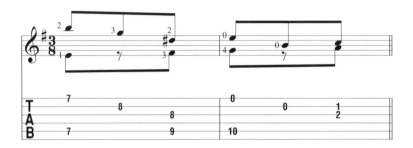

Notice the rest on the second beat of each measure. This requires you to stop the previous notes (E in measure 1 and G in measure 2) from ringing. In cases like this, all you need to do is release pressure from the finger that is fretting the note, thereby cutting off its sound. In some cases, this may take a little practice.

In the instance above, we are muting fretted notes, but you are called upon to mute notes played as open strings, as well. Check out measure 13 below.

MEASURE 13

In order to stop the G note on the second beat, you will need to lightly touch the third string with a fretting-hand finger. This also will take some getting used to.

MORE PERFORMANCE AND PRACTICE NOTES

▶ Play this piece at a moderate tempo with a slight *ritardando* (gradual slowing of the tempo) at the end.

▶ To reinforce the intended playfulness of this piece, experiment with an overall *staccato* feel, making the notes short and detached.

▶ While "Minuetto Scherzando" is supposed to be lively, it also displays the composer's sense of drama (dynamics are a great way to express this). Pay attention to the dynamics indicated in the music, but use them as a springboard for your own interpretation. Keep in mind that a general tendency is to *crescendo* (grow louder) toward the ends of sections.

▶ Rest strokes can also be used for emphasis and variety, like on the first notes of each section or for short runs. Use them sparingly, though, as you want to maintain the overall lightness of the piece.

▶ Some other things to watch out for are the half barre in the second-to-last measure (a B7 chord barred at the second fret) and the pull-offs in measures 4, 12, and 21 (make sure to perform these cleanly and with an even tone).

MINUETTO SCHERZANDO

Alessandro Scarlatti

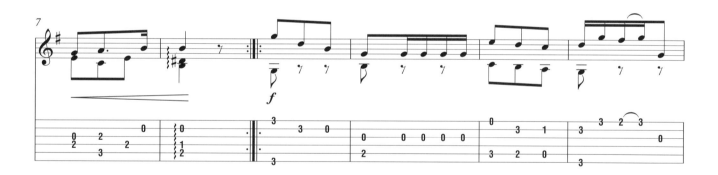

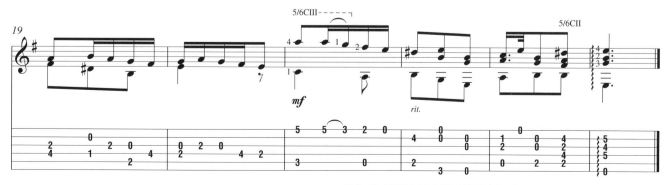

RIGHT-HAND STUDIES (GIULIANI)

Overview

Mauro Giuliani (1781–1829) was an influential virtuoso and composer for classical guitar. Among his lessons for technique development, *120 Right-Hand Studies* stands out. This series of exercises provides an exhaustive look at possible plucking-hand finger combinations. Conveniently, the fretting hand features only two chords, C and G7, and this enables the student to focus on the plucking hand. Because we cannot give all 120 exercises in this lesson, we have included the first 16, and this sampling hints at all the various combinations actually covered by Giuliani. After practicing these first 16 exercises, seek out the others and practice them on your own—but not all at once, as these take time to master (plus, you'll need a break from hearing C to G7 over and over again!).

Performance and Practice Notes

▶ Practice each exercise separately, repeating as many times as necessary until comfortable. After the desired number of repetitions, end with a final C chord (below). You can also try stringing together all the exercises you've mastered.

▶ At first, use *full planting* for all ascending arpeggios and use *sequential planting* for all descending arpeggios. Then, use sequential planting for all, which is what you would use in most practical playing situations. (**Note:** With full planting, the plucking-hand fingers are all positioned on the strings before starting the arpeggio. After the pattern has begun, the *i*, *m*, and *a* fingers are positioned on the strings immediately after the plucking of the *p*. In sequential planting, each finger—*p*, *i*, *m*, and *a*—is positioned on the string immediately prior to plucking.)

RIGHT-HAND STUDIES 1–16

Mauro Giuliani

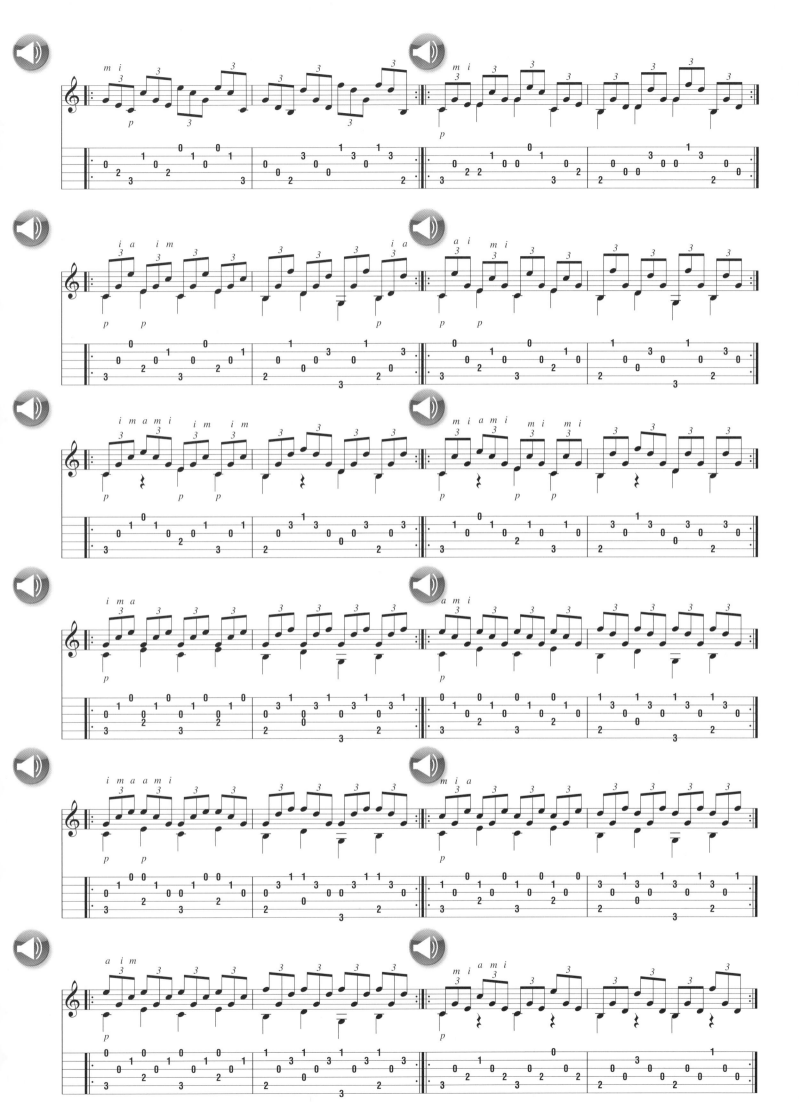

"MINUET IN G MAJOR" (PETZOLD)

Overview

A *minuet* is a musical form that originated from a 17th-century French dance. Minuets were written in triple meter (usually 3/4 or 6/8) and often featured a *binary form*, with both parts repeating.

"Minuet in G Major," which was attributed to J. S. Bach until 1970 but is now credited to Christian Petzold, is a keyboard piece included in the *Notebook for Anna Magdalena Bach* (1725). Anna Magdalena was Bach's second wife, and the book contained works by many composers of the day, including Bach himself.

Thirty-two measures in length, this binary piece consists of two 16-measure parts, each of which is repeated. This minuet is a great example of combining a moving bass line with a melody. The upper voice is a simple, predominantly stepwise melody, and the lower voice, the bass line, jumps around a bit more but also features stepwise runs to be played with the thumb.

Performance and Practice Notes

▸ Practice the upper voice and the lower voice separately so that when you combine them, you know how they are supposed to sound and also have a good grasp of the mechanics required to play them.

▸ Pay attention to the fretting-hand fingerings, as they provide the smoothest and most efficient movement from beat to beat. However, don't feel bound to the fingerings—experiment with your own, as you may find preferable solutions.

▸ Alternate your plucking-hand fingers in the upper voice while plucking the bass notes with your thumb. Avoid letting your thumb dominate the piece. Make sure that the melody is featured prominently.

▸ Experiment with a combination of rest and free strokes. Try using rest strokes on the downbeat of each measure. When you have a feel for this, apply it in a way that sounds best to you. You can even try free strokes the first time through each part and then rest strokes when you repeat.

▸ Be sure to vary your tone and dynamics. Try playing *sul tasto* (near the fretboard) for a warm, full-bodied sound the first time through each part, and then play *sul ponticello* (near the bridge) for a trebly, more biting sound the second time through each part. Experiment with volume, as well, playing one part louder than the other, or the repeats louder than the first iterations of the parts. Your personal interpretation of this piece is key to your personal expression and enjoyment.

▸ The tempo is *andantino*, which is slightly faster than *andante*. Practice the piece slowly and with a steady rhythm at first. Once you have the mechanics down, let the music breath by experimenting with *rubato* (slight deviations from a strict tempo) and brief *fermatas* (holding notes for longer than their written duration).

MINUET IN G MAJOR

Christian Petzold

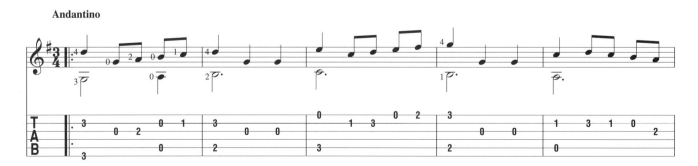

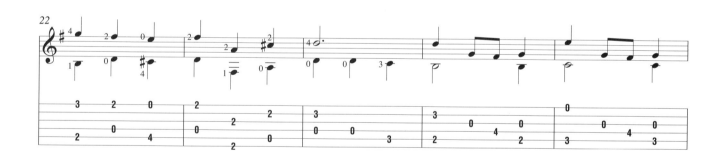

"BOURRÉE IN E MINOR" (BACH)

Overview

"Bourrée" is the fifth movement from J. S. Bach's *Lute Suite No. 1 in E Minor*. This piece is so famous that it has been arranged and adapted by rock legends like Jethro Tull, Yngwie Malmsteen, and Led Zeppelin, among others.

The bourrée was a lively French dance, and though this particular piece was not intended for dancing, it still maintains an animated feel and vigorous rhythm. When performing it, you can be assured that your fingers will be dancing across the fingerboard.

Additionally, "Bourrée" is a great example of *counterpoint*, as it features two independent voices.

Performance and Practice Notes

▶ The tempo is *allegro*, and it should be played at about 120 bpm. Achieving this speed will take time and practice. Concentrate on each measure and section until you have it down pat—only then should you move on.

▶ The left-hand fingering is crucial (though there are many different fingering options, start with the fingerings as written). In many instances, there are full barres (and nearly full barres) that appear only for a single beat. This will require your hand to do a lot of bouncing around. However, the bouncing has been minimized as much as possible by utilizing *guide fingers*. A guide finger remains in contact with the string—but with tension released and no longer pressing against the fingerboard—when shifting to a new position, and it is often the lead note in that new position. Guide fingers help make smoother transitions when shifting. When notated, guide-finger numbers are preceded by dashes (–4, –2, etc.). A great example of how guide fingers can make smooth transitions is found in measures 22–24. Remember: try to avoid squeaking sounds when shifting.

BOURRÉE
(FROM *LUTE SUITE NO. 1 IN E MINOR*)

J. S. Bach

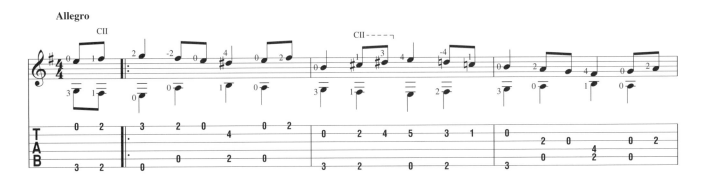

Overview

Fernando Sor (1778–1839) is among the most important composers for guitar. His studies for improving technique and teaching the instrument are not only great exercises, but have become a part of standard guitar repertoire—and Op. 6, No. 8 is no exception. This piece appears as "Estudio 1" in Andrés Segovia's *Studies for Guitar by Fernando Sor*. The following arrangement has slightly different fingerings and dynamic suggestions than Segovia's.

Performance and Practice Notes

▶ The tempo is *adagio*, or slowly and stately, and should be played at about 70 bpm.

▶ Notice there is a third, or middle, voice. Be sure to bring out each voice—think of each as being another instrument. In some places, different dynamics are indicated for various voices; for instance, in measures 19–23, the bass voice and upper voice crescendo at different times. Performing different dynamics in separate voices takes some practice, but it sounds fantastic.

▶ Left-hand fingering is critical in this piece. Many passages would be extremely awkward with fingerings other than those indicated. Try the written fingerings first, then feel free to explore other options.

▶ Watch for the passages with barres, practicing them until comfortable.

▶ Play this piece *legato*, with all the lines smooth, fluid, and connected. Make sure that all the notes ring out for their full value. This will require you to hold certain notes while forming other notes or chords above or below. A great example of this is found in measures 32–39.

STUDY IN C, OP. 6, NO. 8

Fernando Sor

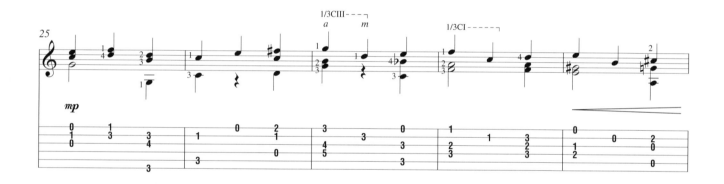

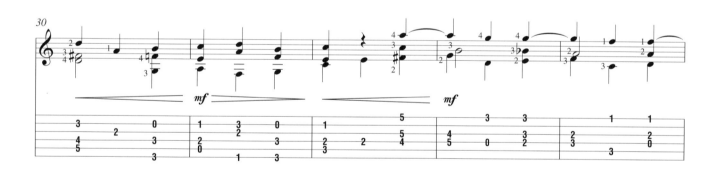

LESSON #46: STUDY IN B MINOR, OP. 35, NO. 22 (SOR)

▶ The tempo is *moderato* and should be played at about 108 bpm.

▶ Perform this piece with a *rubato* feel, slowing down and picking up the tempo according to your personal taste. You will notice the indications *rit.* (slow down) and *a tempo* (return to original tempo). Use these as guides but do not let them limit your personal interpretation.

▶ The intended feel is *legato*, or smooth and connected. Many of the chords are held in place by the fretting hand while the plucking hand sounds the strings. The notes ring harmoniously into each other, creating a tranquil stream of sound.

▶ Be sure to bring out the melody notes in the upper voice (stems pointing upward)—the accompaniment should remain slightly in the background. This will take some practice, as you are plucking both melody and accompaniment with the same hand. (On piano, for instance, separate hands can play the melody and accompaniment.)

▶ It was once the fashion to play the melody with rest strokes, but the trend now is to keep it relatively light by using only free strokes. Experiment with both!

▶ There many barres in this piece, including a couple of full barres (measures 32–34 and 47). Practice these until comfortable. At times, it is necessary to finger a barre, in preparation, before it is actually needed. For example, when transitioning from measure 39 to measure 40, it is necessary to place your first finger across the top four strings on beat 1 so that when you pull your third finger off on beat 3, the barre is already in place to play the E and C♯.

STUDY IN B MINOR, OP. 35, NO. 22

Fernando Sor

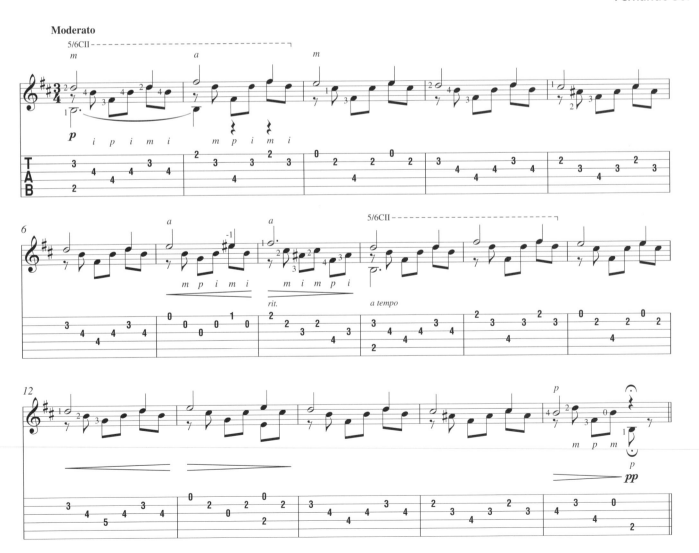

Overview

A staple in classical guitar repertoire, "Romanza" is a traditional 19th-century Spanish ballad. It has a three-part form: the first part is in E minor, the second part is in the parallel major key (E major), and the last part is a restatement of the minor section. Here is your "road map" for the piece:

1. Play the first part (measures 1–16), and then repeat it.

2. Play the second part (measure 17–32), and then repeat it.

3. *D.C. al Fine*, or go back to the beginning and play until the *Fine*.

Performance and Practice Notes

▶ The tempo is *andantino* and is to be played at about 90 bpm. A *rubato* feel—slowing and then picking up the tempo at appropriate places throughout—works well with this piece. Experiment by applying rubato in places of your choosing, and then listen to the audio for additional ideas.

▶ "Romanza" features a treble melody over an arpeggio accompaniment. Strive to bring out the melody and make it sing. You can accomplish this by accenting the melody notes (played by the *a* finger) and by liberally applying vibrato to them.

▶ There are quite a few position shifts in this piece, many of which shift to a different position on the same string, using the same finger. This is indicated with a dash preceding the finger number (–2, –3, etc.). This type of shift occurs in measures 2, 4, 11, 14, etc. Be sure to make a clean shift, releasing tension with your fretting-hand finger before you slide to the new position. There are also more drastic position shifts, as in measures 9 and 21. Practice these shifts slowly and as many times as it takes to make them clean and seamless.

▶ Finally, play expressively—with dynamics, feeling, and variation in tone color. This is a romantic ballad—play it like one!

ROMANZA

Anonymous

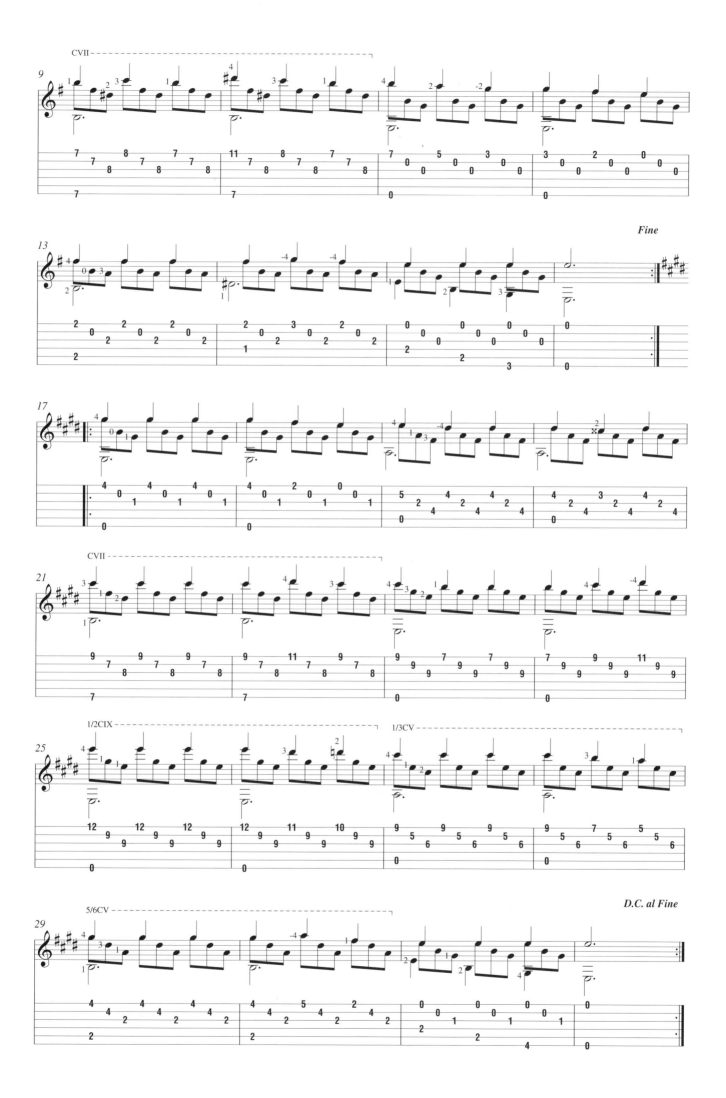

LESSON #48: "SPAGNOLETTA"

Overview

Spagnoletta is Italian for the Spanish *españoleta,* which was a Spanish dance in triple meter. Both terms also refer to the music accompanying the dance. There were many compositions, by either the Italian or Spanish name, that were very similar to the one we will be learning. For example, "Españoleta," by Gaspar Sanz, shares a similar rhythm and melody. Check out the first several measures below.

MEASURES 1–7 OF "ESPAÑOLETA" BY GASPAR SANZ

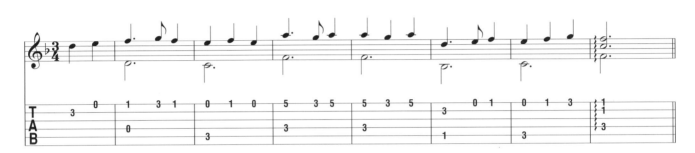

"Spagnoletta" (Anonymous) was first transcribed from the early lute tablature in *Lautenspieler des XVI. Jahrhunderts* by Oscar Chilesotti (1848–1916). His transcription can be played on the guitar without adaptation, though we have made a minor change or two to suit the purposes of our lesson.

THE PICARDY 3RD

The *Picardy 3rd* was a standard practice of the Renaissance and early Baroque periods of ending a section or entire piece on a major chord when the rest of the composition was predominantly minor. For instance, when a piece is in the key of A minor (as is much of "Spagnoletta"), it ends with an A *major* chord rather than an A minor chord. The Picardy 3rd refers to the raising of the minor 3rd in the tonic chord. So, if the tonic chord is A minor (A–C–E), we would raise the 3rd of the chord, changing it from a minor 3rd to a major 3rd, and thereby turning the chord into an A major chord (A–C♯–E). This practice gave even melancholy pieces (which were prevalent during the Renaissance) a "happy" or "hopeful" ending. In "Spagnoletta," notice the Picardy 3rds in measures 15 and 25.

Performance and Practice Notes

▶ Our tempo is *allegro* and should be played at somewhere around 120 bpm. The piece should be played with a light, gentle feel.

▶ Note the half barre in measure 5. This is a standard first-position F chord. Make sure your transitions from chords to double stops to chords are played cleanly in this measure and throughout the piece.

▶ Measure 15 includes a five-note chord. The roll symbol ⟨ tells you to strum the notes separately. So, in this case, you will strum the bottom two notes with your thumb. You can choose to pluck the top three notes of the chord simultaneously or roll the entire chord.

▶ Measure 18 marks the beginning of a new section. You can distinguish it by placing a rest stroke on the downbeat, or you can alter the tone by playing *sul ponticello* (near the bridge) or *sul tasto* (near the fretboard), depending on your tone in the previous section.

SPAGNOLETTA

Anonymous

LESSON #49: "ALMAN" (JOHNSON)

Overview

Lutenist and composer Robert Johnson (c. 1583–c. 1634) was the son of John Johnson, lutenist in the court of Queen Elizabeth I. Robert worked with playwright William Shakespeare on some of his later plays and has the distinction of being the only known composer to have composed original music to Shakespeare's lyrics for the original productions.

An *alman* is the same as an *allemande* and was a popular dance of the Renaissance and Baroque periods.

Performance and Practice Notes

▶ "Alman" has a lively feel and should be played at about 108 bpm.

▶ Measures 17–32 feature some challenging finger work. Be sure to break this section down into subsections and master the fingering before moving on.

▶ Measures 17, 18, 25, and 26 feature *hinge barres*. A hinge barre is a technique whereby a finger frets a single string and then drops to form a barre while still holding the original string. "Alman" has several "half" hinge barres in which two-string barres are formed. In this book, hinge barres are notated with "HB," so you will see "1/3HB" followed by position indicators (Roman numerals) above measures 17, 18, 25, and 26.

ALMAN

Robert Johnson

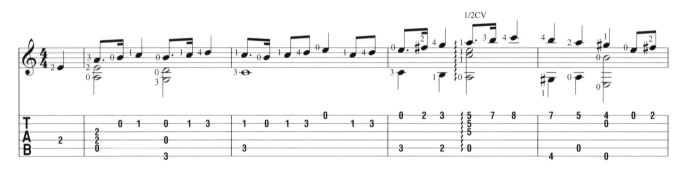

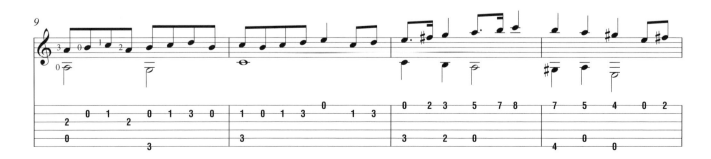

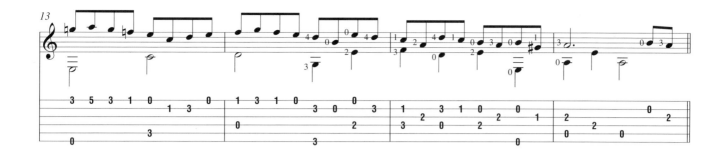

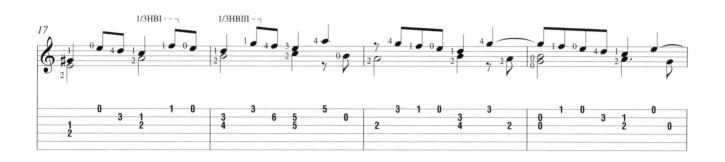

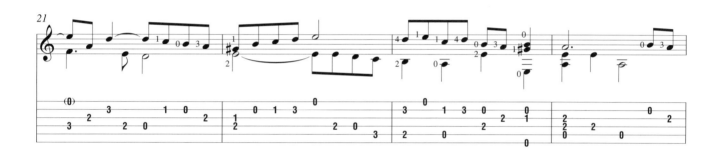

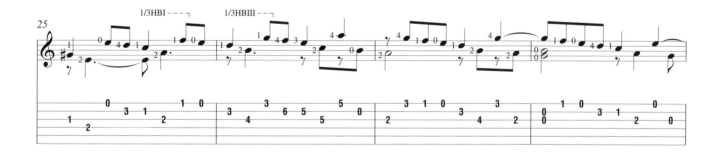

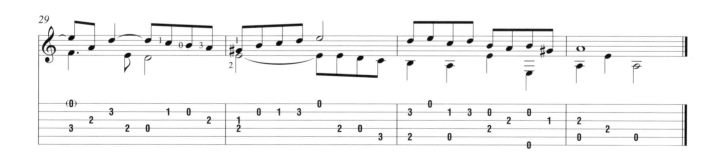

LESSON #50: CHORD INVERSIONS

A chord is an *inversion* when the lowest note is a chord tone other than the root. (**Note:** When the root is the lowest tone, the chord is in *root position*.) When the 3rd is the lowest tone, the chord is in *first inversion*; when the 5th is the lowest tone, the chord is in *second inversion*, etc. The number of inversions depends on the number of chord tones.

Triads

Triads have two inversions: first inversion (3rd in the bass) and second inversion (5th in the bass). Let's look at the inversions of a C major triad.

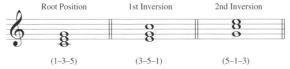

Now let's play inversion examples on four different string sets (1–2–3, 2–3–4, 3–4–5, and 4–5–6). Pluck the chords with either *i–m–a* or *p–i–m*.

C MAJOR INVERSIONS (STRINGS 1–2–3)

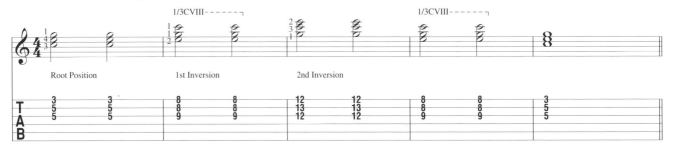

G MAJOR INVERSIONS (STRINGS 2–3–4)

D MAJOR INVERSIONS (STRINGS 3–4–5)

A MAJOR INVERSIONS (STRINGS 4–5–6)

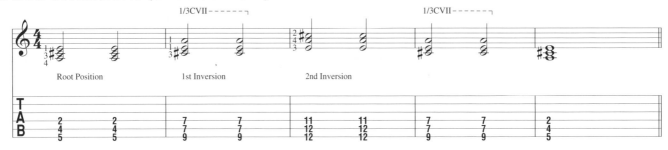

Of course, you can go through all the minor-triad inversions, as well, just by lowering the 3rd of each chord by a half step.

Seventh Chords

Because seventh chords have four chord tones, there are three inversions: first inversion (3rd in the bass), second inversion (5th in the bass), and *3rd inversion* (7th in the bass). Let's look at the inversions of a G7 chord.

Now let's play inversion examples on three different string sets (1–2–3–4, 2–3–4–5, and 3–4–5–6). Note that, to be a particular inversion, it is essential to start with the right chord tone. However, the other tones in the voicing can be in any order. For example, the first inversion of E7 below features a 3–♭7–1–5 order. This qualifies as a first inversion because it has the 3rd as its lowest note. Play and memorize the following inversions.

E7 INVERSIONS (STRINGS 1–2–3–4)

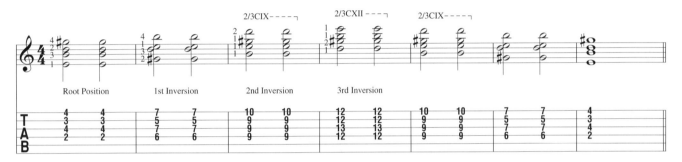

B♭7 INVERSIONS (STRINGS 2–3–4–5)

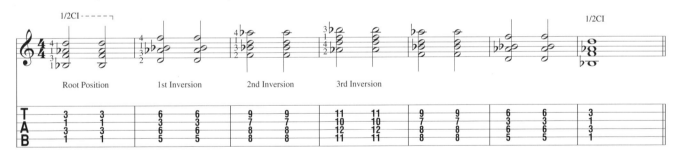

F7 INVERSIONS (STRINGS 3–4–5–6)

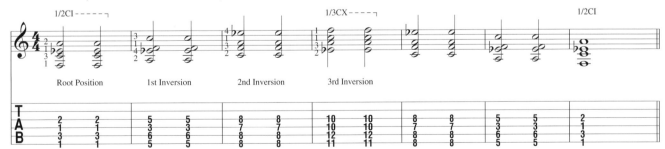

Of course, you can go through all other seventh-chord inversions, as well, just by adjusting the appropriate tones. For example, to play all the major-seventh inversions, just raise the 7th of each chord by a half step.

LESSON #51: TUNING YOUR GUITAR

According to Baroque music theorist/composer Johann Mattheson (1681–1764): "If a lutenist lives to be 80 years old, surely he has spent 60 years tuning." Many guitarists would agree. Let's explore effective ways of tuning our instruments.

Electronic Tuners

Free-standing electronic tuners work well, as do apps for smart phones and tablets.

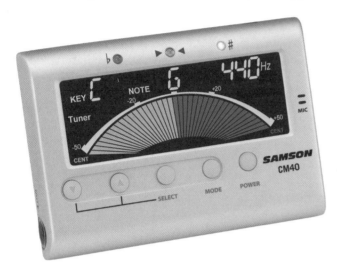

Contact tuners, which sense the vibrations of your guitar's strings rather than hearing the pitches, work best in noisy rooms or rehearsals where many instrumentalists are tuning at once.

Before using your electronic tuner, check to see if it is a *chromatic tuner* or a *guitar tuner*. Chromatic tuners will register *all* notes (naturals and accidentals). For example, they will indicate whether you're playing a slightly sharp F♯ or if you are closer to a G. A guitar tuner will only detect the pitches of the six strings on the guitar: E, A, D, G, B, and E. The tuner roughly identifies which of the six open strings is closest to the pitch you are playing and tells you if you are higher or lower than the pitch.

contact tuner

Relative Tuning Revisited

Many guitarists first learn to tune by matching a fretted note on one string to the next open string:

▶ Open fifth string to the sixth string, fifth fret

▶ Open fourth string to the fifth string, fifth fret

▶ Open third string to the fourth string, fifth fret

▶ Open second string to the third string, fourth fret

▶ Open first string to the second string, fifth fret

Although we've all used this system, it rarely gets the instrument perfectly in tune. A slight mistake when tuning any lower string is magnified as you progress to the higher strings.

Matching each string to a stable, identical pitch is the most effective and accurate way to tune:

1. Start with the open first string E

2. Match the E on the second string, fifth fret to the open E

3. Match the E on the third string, ninth fret to the open E

4. Match the E (one octave lower) on the fourth string, second fret with the open E.

5. Match the E (one octave lower) on the fifth string, seventh fret—or seventh-fret harmonic (same octave)—with the open E

6. Match the open sixth-string E (two octaves lower), the 12th-fret harmonic (one octave lower), or the fifth-fret harmonic (same octave) to the open E

Confirm that your guitar is in tune by playing the following chord, one note at a time. You'll notice that there is no 3rd in the chord, only octaves and 5ths.

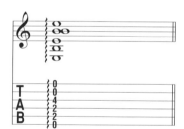

Strings

Occasionally, a string may not be "true." This happens whenever there is an inconsistency in the diameter of the vibrating string length. To check that your strings are true, play the 12th-fret harmonic of the suspected string and compare it to the 12th-fret fretted note. The pitches should be exactly the same, even though the tone quality is different. Similarly, the note produced by the seventh-fret harmonic should be the same pitch as the fretted seventh fret, one octave higher.

Tuning Tips

When tuning, always approach a pitch from below. The string needs to be slightly loosened and then tightened again in order to stay in tune. Even if the string is only slightly sharp, pass the correct pitch on the way down, and then approach the pitch from below.

Play a "pure" pitch when tuning. Avoid the use of vibrato and make sure that your left hand is directly on top of the fretted string, not inadvertently pulling the string down or pushing it up.

LESSON #52: SITTING POSITION AND POSTURE

A comfortable and relaxed playing position is essential for effective classical guitar performance.

Your fretting hand must have full access to all positions on the fretboard. Your plucking hand needs to remain relaxed, comfortable, and stable while playing all six strings. Your upper body, neck, shoulders, and back remain relaxed and ready for action. Your lower body provides a stable base from which to play.

A good sitting position for guitar creates four contact points between you and the guitar:

1. The guitar rests on your left upper thigh
2. The guitar is supported by your right inner thigh
3. The back of the guitar tilts back to contact your sternum
4. Your right forearm rests lightly on the side of the guitar

The height of the chair or bench is important. When you sit toward the front of the chair, your feet should fall comfortably on the floor. If the chair is too high, it will be difficult to support the guitar. If the chair is too short, your legs may bow outward and/or you will experience stress on your lower back.

Traditionally, classical guitarists have used a *footstool* to raise their left leg and support the guitar in good playing position. Place the footstool just to the left of center. Adjust the height of the footstool so that when raised, your left upper thigh is at a right angle to the floor. If your upper thigh slopes downward, so will the guitar.

You may find that using a footstool is uncomfortable. Don't fret—devices are available to support your guitar while keeping both legs on the ground. The ErgoPlay, A-Frame, Guitar Pillow, and Gitano Support are a few devices invented to raise your guitar into a good sitting position without the use of a footstool.

Some guitarists find that using a lower footstool along with a supportive device provides them with the best sitting position. Be sure to experiment and find what works for you.

Sit with a straight back and relaxed shoulders. Place the center of the guitar (about the 12th or 13th fret) in the middle of your body.

The guitar neck is raised to about a 45-degree angle. The E string tuning peg is at about eye level.

Maintain a space between your body and the guitar. Rather than holding the guitar perpendicular to the ground, let the guitar tilt backward. This places the upper bout of the guitar in contact with your sternum. Angling the soundhole upward helps with sound projection. Keeping the guitar away from your body prevents your belly from damping the vibrations of the guitar.

Avoid the "guitarist twist." Keep the guitar neck/fretboard in front of your shoulder and avoid twisting to the left. Try this exercise: Raise your left hand up as if you were fretting a note in first position. Open and close your fist, keeping your hand slightly in front of your body. Now open and close your fist with your hand parallel to your shoulder. You'll feel more control and strength in your left hand when it is in front of you. For a great sitting position, keep the right side of the guitar closer to your body and the guitar neck a little in front of you. In this position, you will not have a complete view of your fingers on the fretboard. That's OK! Keep your head and neck aligned, turning only your head slightly to the left. You'll be able to see the edge of the frets and which frets your fingers are playing. That's all the information you really need.

Some guitarists find that the instrument slips off their legs as they are playing. Non-slip, non-adhesive shelf liner provides an easy fix. Place a small square of the cloth between your right and left leg where the guitar or guitar support rests. The guitar will stay comfortably in place.

LESSON #53: "ADELITA" (TÁRREGA)

"Adelita," by Francisco Tárrega (1852–1909), is a short character piece first published in 1902 by *Antich y Tena*, a publishing house in Valencia, Spain. Labeled a "mazurka," "Adelita" is often performed together with Tárrega's beautiful short piece "Lágrima."

"Adelita" opens with a descending melodic motif that spans an interval of a 4th. In measures 2–3, the motif is transposed down in whole steps and, in measure 4, the melodic interval expands. Practice the treble line alone and learn to express Tárrega's beautiful melody before adding the bass line.

MEASURES 1–4 (MELODY ONLY)

The small notes in measures 4, 11, 12, and 14 are grace notes. Play the first note of the ornament on the beat, slurring the subsequent two pitches. The first grace note of the figure is played with the bass. Grace notes are played as fast as possible, taking away little or no time from the main note. Many editors have changed the notation of these ornaments, but Tárrega's original notation (version 2) best communicates the importance of the main note.

MEASURE 4 WRITTEN TWO DIFFERENT WAYS

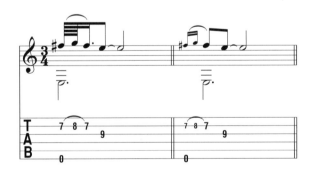

ADELITA

Francisco Tárrega

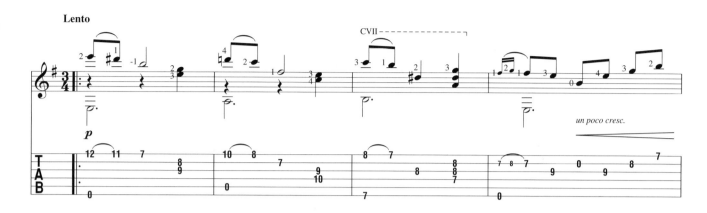

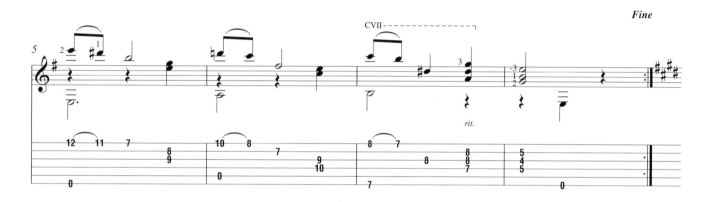

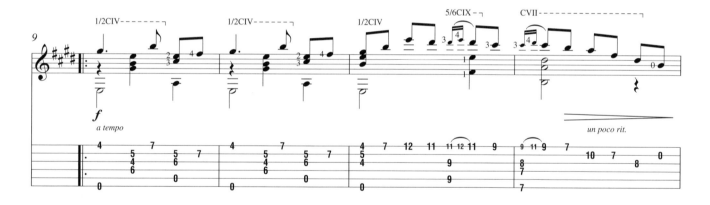

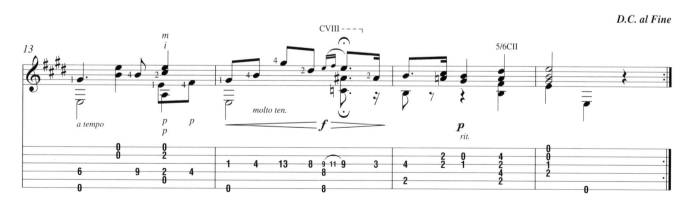

LESSON #54: ARTIFICIAL HARMONICS

Natural harmonics are played on the guitar at the 12th, seventh, and fifth frets. Harmonics at the 12th fret sound one octave higher than the open string, harmonics on the seventh fret sound one octave plus a 5th above the open string, and harmonics on the fifth fret sound two octaves higher than the open string.

Artificial harmonics, or "harp harmonics," provide the opportunity to play any note of the chromatic scale as a harmonic. To play an artificial harmonic, we must touch the string exactly in the middle of its vibrating length. Touching the *node* at the midway point divides the vibrating string length in half and creates a harmonic an octave above the original pitch. Twelve frets from any fretted note is the midway point, or node, of the vibrating string length.

To play the harmonic F, fret the first string, first fret as normal. Extend your right-hand index finger and lightly touch the string directly above the 13th-fret wire. Pluck the note with your *annular* finger (*a*, or ring finger), separating it as far from the index finger as possible. Your thumb can stabilize your hand by gently resting on one of the bass strings.

EXAMPLE 1

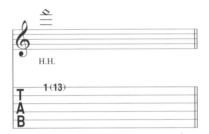

An alternate approach to playing artificial harmonics starts with extending your right-hand index finger and lightly touching the string directly above the fret. But in this method, you pluck the note with your thumb, bending it to cross underneath your index finger.

This technique works fine for single-note harmonics but, to play artificial harmonics along with a bass note, you must use the first method, as in this example.

EXAMPLE 2

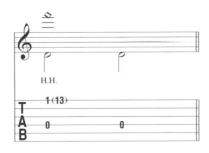

Play the following chromatic scale using artificial harmonics. Fret the pitches as normal with your left hand, lightly touching your right-hand index finger above the fret wire, 12 frets higher than the fretted note.

EXAMPLE 3

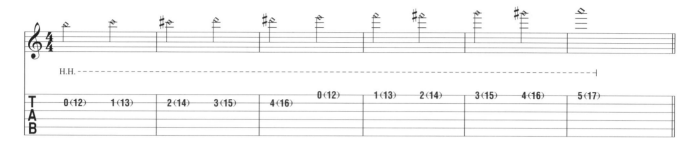

Playing artificial harmonics past the fifth fret is more difficult because we run out of fret wire over which to place the right hand. It's still possible to create an artificial harmonic, however. Visualize above the soundboard the location of the next, higher fret and lightly touch it with your index finger. If you're in the right spot, you'll hear a beautiful harmonic.

EXAMPLE 4

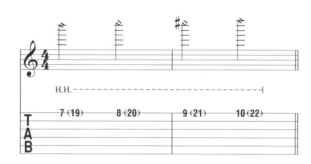

Miguel Llobet (1878–1938) used artificial harmonics in his beautiful Catalonian folk song "El Testament d' Amelia."

EXAMPLE 5

LESSON #55: ASCENDING ARPEGGIOS

The secret to playing beautiful, strong, and fast arpeggios is placing your plucking-hand fingers on the strings just prior to plucking the notes. You don't have to linger on the string long to get the benefits. Just an instant of contact with the string before you play will help improve your tone, accuracy, and speed.

Planting, or full preparation, although not always used in performance, is a technique that will help you develop your right-hand free stroke and improve your ascending arpeggios.

Full Preparation

Before playing an ascending arpeggio, place, or plant, all pluck-hand fingers used in the arpeggio on the strings. As your thumb plays the bass note, all fingers used in the arpeggio lightly touch their strings. The beginning of a fully planted arpeggio feels like playing a chord.

Using full preparation to play an arpeggio like this:

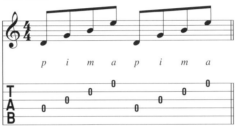

Feels like this:

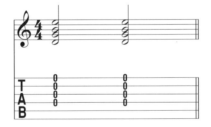

Your fingers touch each string on the contact point (i.e., the exact point from which you play). Avoid placing your finger on the fleshy part, then rolling to the nail. That takes too much time. Instead, make contact with the string at the very tip of the finger so that the string is touching mostly fingernail, and only a slight bit of flesh. Just prior to playing each note, push the string in, then play. As you play or release the string, your finger immediately relaxes. Each finger remains on the string until it plays.

In the following exercise, place *p*, *i*, *m*, and *a* fingers on the strings at the beginning of the arpeggio.

▸ *Pulgar* (thumb) plays while the index, middle, and *annular* (ring) fingers remain on the strings.

▸ Index plays while middle and annular fingers stay put.

▸ Middle plays; annular finger remains on the string and then plays.

EXAMPLE 1

Only plant the fingers that are on the ascending portion of the arpeggio. In this example, plant only index and annular.

EXAMPLE 2

In the example below, plant *p*, *i*, *m*, and *a* fingers at the start of the ascending arpeggio.

EXAMPLE 3

Planting works well at the beginning of a piece or section when it doesn't matter if the previous sonorities are cut off by your right-hand fingers coming into contact with the strings early. It's extremely helpful in arpeggio passages that change patterns or move to different sets of strings.

EXAMPLE 4

EXAMPLE 5

Even though planting is an effective performance tool and, with regular practice, will develop right-hand strength, finger independence, and accuracy, planting has its disadvantages:

> ▶ It's only applicable to ascending patterns.

> ▶ Previously played pitches are cut off.

> ▶ The technique does not work well at fast tempos.

Practice planting to develop your technique. Also explore *sequential preparation*, or placing individual right-hand fingers on the string immediately before playing.

LESSON #56: ASCENDING SLURS

A *slur* is notated as a curved line that connects two or more notes and instructs the musician to play the notes smoothly, or *legato*. On a bowed instrument like a violin or cello, the notes under the slur are played within a single bow movement. On a wind instrument like a flute or saxophone, the slurred notes are played in one breath, without separate articulations.

To play a slur on the guitar, pluck the first note of the slur, then use only the left hand to articulate the notes under the slur marking.

Ascending slurs are also called "hammer-ons" by folk and pop guitarists. It's an accurate name because in order to play an ascending slur, you pluck the first note, then tap, or hammer onto, the following note(s).

The basic motion of the ascending slur is the same motion that you use to roll your finger on the table as you patiently—or not so patiently—wait for your morning coffee.

Try it. You'll notice that the motion for tapping the table comes from your large knuckles (metacarpophalangeal joints). You'll also notice that once your finger hits the surface of the table, it relaxes. The weight of your finger continues to rest on the table, but you don't exert any pressure. This is just like playing an ascending slur.

EXERCISE 1

Let's start by practicing a four-finger simultaneous tap, or hammer-on, at the fifth fret. Tap fingers 1, 2, 3, and 4 simultaneously on the string. Start with the sixth string and progress through the remaining five strings. As soon as you hit the string, relax your fingers and let the weight of your hand sustain the pitch.

This is not the most musical exercise, but it trains your fingers to tap and then release.

EXERCISE 2

Now tap the fingers individually. Tap the first finger onto the string, relax the finger, and keep contact with the string. Now tap fingers 2, 3, and 4. After tapping each finger, relax the pressure while keeping the finger on the string. Remember: this entire exercise is played only with the left hand. Keep all lower fingers on the string until you change strings.

EXERCISE 3

Let's practice a similar exercise, using slurs with fingers 1 and 3, then 2 and 4. Tap finger 1, relax the finger, and keep it on the string, then tap finger 3, relax, and release both fingers 1 and 3. Next, tap finger 2, relax the finger, and stay on the string, then tap finger 4, relax, and release both fingers. Repeat on the next string. Don't play the pitches with the right hand; just tap with your left. You may not produce a lot of sound, but that's OK. Study the movement of your left hand and work for efficient placement on the fretboard—without extraneous motion.

EXERCISE 4

Finally, let's put it all together. Articulate the first note of each slur, then tap, or hammer-on, the second note. The second note will be softer than the first—that's part of the charm of the technique. Play the exercise on the fifth fret, then shift down to the fourth, third, second, and first positions.

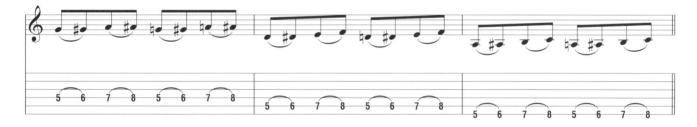

EXERCISE 5

LESSON #57: DESCENDING ARPEGGIOS

Preparation is the technique of placing your right-hand fingers on the strings just prior to plucking the notes. *Planting*, or full preparation, is the technique of placing all of your right-hand fingers on the strings at the beginning of an ascending arpeggio. Planting is a valuable tool that will help you develop your right-hand free stroke and improve your ascending arpeggios. However, planting has its limitations:

▶ It's only used on ascending arpeggio patterns.

▶ Planting cuts off/damps previously played pitches.

▶ The technique is cumbersome at fast tempos.

Use *sequential* preparation to perform descending arpeggios, *legato* sections in which all notes are sustained, and fast arpeggio sections. With sequential preparation, your right-hand finger gets to the string immediately after the previous finger plays. The sooner you arrive on the string, the faster the tempo at which you can play.

Imagine that your fingers are made of very thin metal and the strings are strong magnets. Your fingers are attracted to the strings. They move quickly and touch the string at the contact point. The contact point is the exact spot on each finger from which you release the string. It's usually on the left side of the fingertip where nail and flesh meet.

In the following arpeggio pattern, as soon as *pulgar* (thumb) plays the bass note, the *annular* (ring) finger touches the first string. The annular finger plays and then the middle immediately arrives on the second string. As soon as the middle finger releases the string, the index finger makes contact with the third string. Practice the pattern slowly, exaggerating the preparation of each finger. Once your fingers are consistently arriving at the strings early, speed up the exercise. Only play as fast as you can prepare your fingers on the next string.

EXAMPLE 1

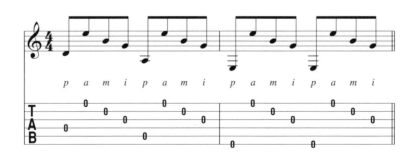

Sequential preparation is like walking on a thin balance beam. As soon as one foot lifts, the next is on the beam. Stay in contact with the beam and you'll successfully walk to the other side. Similarly, after you release one finger, have the next right-hand finger in contact with a string and ready to play.

Use sequential preparation to perform this difficult arpeggio, which is similar to a pattern used in a study by the Cuban composer Leo Brouwer. Place each right-hand finger on the string as soon as the previous note is played. Notice that the annular finger moves from the first string to the second string at the beginning of beat 3. For an accurate performance, prepare the annular finger on the second string early.

EXAMPLE 2

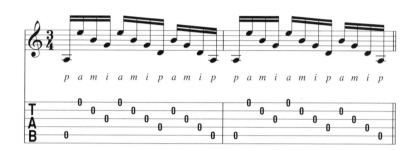

Perhaps one of the most difficult arpeggio patterns in the classical guitar repertoire, the following example is similar to that found in Heitor Villa-Lobos's *Twelve Etudes*. Practice the pattern slowly and exaggerate your preparation of the next note. As you increase the speed, make sure that your fingers still arrive on the string just before you play.

EXAMPLE 3

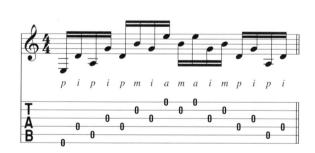

LESSON #58: DESCENDING SLURS

A *slur* is notated as a curved line that connects two or more notes and instructs the musician to play the notes smoothly, or *legato*. On a bowed instrument like a violin or cello, the notes under the slur are played within a single bow movement. On a wind instrument like a flute or saxophone, the slurred notes are played in one breath, without separate articulations.

To play a slur on the guitar, pluck the first note, then use only the left hand to articulate the notes under the slur marking.

Descending slurs are also called "pull-offs" by folk and pop guitarists. It's an accurate name because, to play a descending slur, you pluck the first note with your right hand, then your left hand finger pulls off of the first pitch, sounding the second, lower note of the slur.

A descending slur is like a left-hand rest stroke. When you play a descending slur on the third string, your finger will move downward and come to rest/touch the second string. This downward snap ensures a strong sound. In the context of a piece, it may not always be possible to rest your finger on the next, higher string. In such cases, be sure to use the same downward motion; just avoid touching the next, higher string.

Move only your finger to play a descending slur. Keep your wrist and palm still. Play in rhythm, but when it is time to play the slur, make a quick and deliberate movement.

To play the following exercise, articulate the first note of the slur with your right hand, then use only your left-hand finger to pull off the string and sound the open pitch. Repeat on each string.

EXERCISE 1

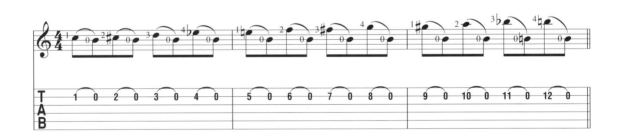

Most often, you'll be performing a descending slur between two fretted notes. Place both fingers on the string before you play the first note of the slur. Avoid bending the lower pitch as you pull off from the higher note. It may help to think about pushing the finger on the lower pitch towards the ceiling at the moment your higher finger pulls off. Start the next exercise in ninth position and work your way down the fretboard.

Maintain good control over all your fingers as you practice these slurs. The fourth finger is the most difficult to control. Work to keep it relaxed and hovering over the fretboard while the other fingers play the slurs.

EXERCISE 2

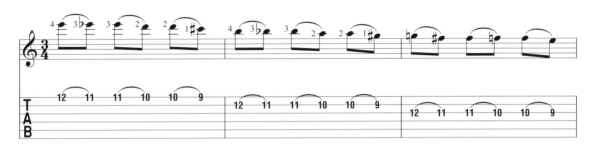

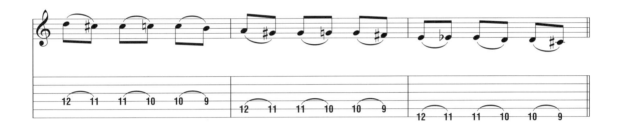

EXERCISE 3

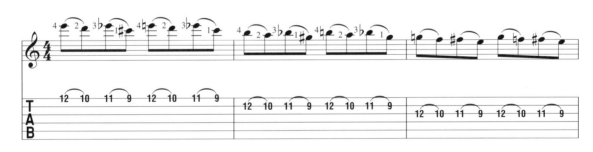

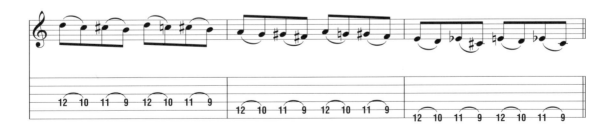

LESSON #59: EXTENDED TECHNIQUES

In addition to creating beautiful tones by playing the strings with rest stroke, free stroke, and strumming, composers and guitarists are developing and using new approaches to produce sound and extend contemporary guitar technique.

Traditional Extended Techniques

HARMONICS

Natural harmonics occur on the 12th, seventh, and fifth fret. Straighten your fret-hand fourth finger and place it directly over the fret wire. Touch the strings lightly, without applying any pressure. As you play each note, lift your left-hand finger from the string, and the sound will amplify.

Artificial harmonics, or "harp harmonics," are created by touching the string 12 frets above the fretted note as you pluck the pitch. When you do this, you will produce a pitch one octave higher than the fretted note.

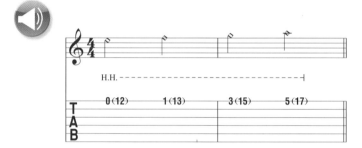

GLISSANDO (OR PORTAMENTO)

Glissando connects two pitches on the same string by sliding the left hand up or down the fretboard. Maintain left-hand pressure so that all intervening pitches are heard.

TAMBOUR

Tambour involves hitting the guitar string with your right hand. Play open strings or fretted notes.

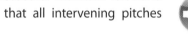

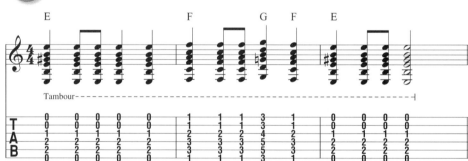

GOLPE

Golpe involves hitting the top, side, or back of the guitar.

PIZZICATO

As you play the fretted notes, damp the strings with your right-hand palm, just in front of the bridge. Electric guitarists call this technique a *palm mute*.

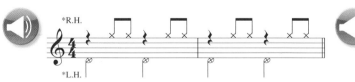

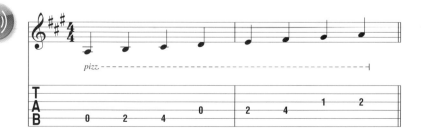

Non-Traditional Extended Techniques

BARTÓK PIZZICATO

Fret the note as normal. Hold the string between your right-hand thumb and index finger. Pull the string out and away from the fingerboard and release it, allowing the string to snap against the frets.

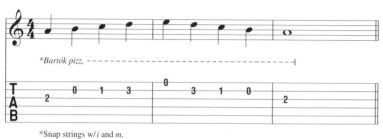

DRUM ROLL

Cross the sixth string over the fifth string with the left-hand finger. Strike the strings simultaneously. As the crossed strings rattle against the fret wires, the resultant sound will replicate a drum roll.

SHIMMER EFFECT

Fret a chord or single note. Rub your right-hand fingertips across the strings as quickly as possible.

WIND MILL

Scratch the string above the nut with your nails or a pick. Don't fret any strings, as it will not change the pitch.

PREPARED GUITAR

Damp the strings by inserting cardboard or cloth underneath or between the strings. Experiment with different materials to create different sound qualities.

Think outside the box and develop your own extended guitar techniques. You'll never know what you might come up with!

LESSON #60: PERCUSSIVE TECHNIQUE—GOLPE

Golpe, the Spanish word for knock, tap, or hit, is a flamenco guitar playing technique that often appears in classical guitar repertoire. To play a golpe, hit the wood of the guitar. You can hit the soundboard, the bridge, and the side or back of the guitar. Dampen the strings while performing the golpe to produce a dry sound or let the strings ring to produce a loud, percussive sound accompanied by a softer pitch.

Non-pitched percussive techniques can be notated different ways. Here, the notehead is replaced with an "X" and written above or below the staff. Dampen the strings with your left hand and tap the bridge of the guitar with your thumb or your fingers to get a dry knock.

EXAMPLE 1

*Tap the bridge with your thumb or fingers.

Tap the lower bout of the guitar with your thumb or fingers (avoid your fingernails) to get a deeper sound.

EXAMPLE 2

*Tap the lower bout with your thumb or fingers.

Tap the upper bout of the guitar to produce a higher-pitched sound.

EXAMPLE 3

*Tap the upper bout with your fingers.

To play this next example, open your right-hand palm and lay it across the strings. Tap the upper bout with your right-hand fingers and the side of the guitar with your left hand.

EXERCISE 4

*Lay R.H. palm across strings, tapping upper bout w/ the fingers. L.H. taps side of guitar.

Let the open strings ring or fret a chord and you'll add pitch to these percussive techniques:

EXAMPLE 5

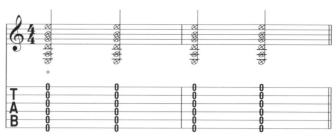

*Tap lower bout w/ thumb or fingers to sound open strings.

EXAMPLE 6

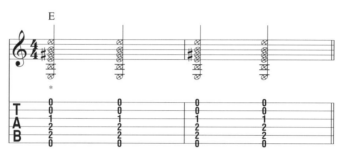

*Tap the bridge w/ your thumb to sound chord.

Try tapping the guitar with your fingertips, knuckles, and thumb. Each produces a different sound. Often, composers specifically notate where on the guitar and how to play a golpe. Other times, it's up to you to find the specific sound.

Listen to *Bordel 1900,* the first movement of Astor Piazzola's *Histoire du Tango* for flute and guitar. The movement begins with the guitarist performing a golpe.

Flamenco players may perform a golpe together with a pitched note. They will play a bass note with the thumb while using their fingernails to strike the soundboard. It's a dangerous move. Don't try it unless you don't mind scratching your guitar or have a golpeador/tap-plate protecting the soundboard.

For a classical guitar example similar to this flamenco technique, listen to *Ostinato*, the second movement from *Elogio de la Danza* by Leo Brouwer. Brouwer indicates *golpe sobre el puente* ("strike the bridge") at the same time the performer plays a low E.

If you would like to hear more pitch with percussive technique, try using the tambour. It's similar to the golpe, except when playing the tambour, you hit the strings, not the wood of the guitar.

PERCUSSIVE TECHNIQUE— TAMBOUR

Tambour (French), or *tambor* (Spanish), is a classical and flamenco guitar technique in which a pitch is produced by striking the guitar strings.

The tambour can be played to produce the sound of the open strings, a chord, or just a few notes. It is similar to the golpe technique, but when playing the tambour, you hit the strings, not the wood of the guitar.

To play the tambour, strike the strings with the boney part of your right-hand thumb. Keep your thumb straight and parallel to the bridge so you can reach all six strings if desired. Keep your arm in contact with the guitar as in normal playing position. Rotate your forearm to the right, then quickly twist back, hitting the strings with your thumb. Move fast and stay loose. Once you make contact, allow your thumb to bounce off the strings.

Strike the strings between the soundhole and the bridge. The strings are tauter near the bridge. Hit close to the bridge, and you'll produce more of the pitch.

The tambour may be notated in the score with an "X" used in place of the notehead. You may also find pitches written as normal, with the instructions "tambour," "tambor," or "tam." indicated underneath the staff.

OPEN-STRING TAMBOUR

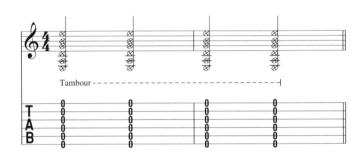

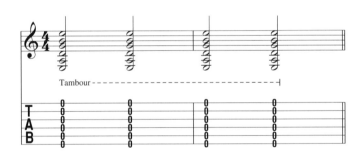

COMMON-CHORD TAMBOUR

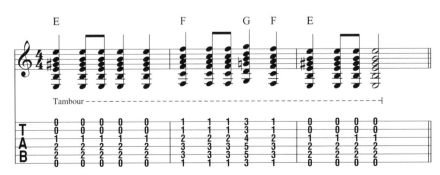

BASS-MELODY TAMBOUR

Adjust your position so that the thumb hits the bottom two strings, avoiding the treble notes.

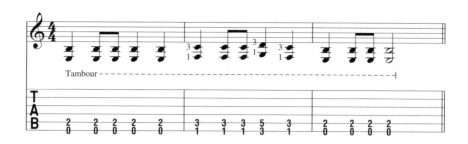

Fandanguillo by Joaquin Turina (1882–1949) is a great example of this technique. The piece begins with a tambour played on just strings 6–5.

HARMONIZED-MELODY TAMBOUR

This technique works best if the melody is limited to only the top two strings. When the melody is on the second string, adjust your position, sliding your right hand so that your thumb misses the first string.

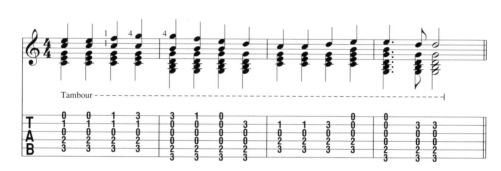

"Aconquija," from *Suite Andina* by the great Paraguayan guitarist and composer Agustìn Barrios Mangore, includes a 16-measure harmonized melody played entirely with tambour.

The previous examples are played by striking the strings between the soundhole and bridge with your right hand to bring out pitch. Strings are tighter near the bridge and looser inside and above the soundhole. Slap the strings near the fretboard, and you'll produce a brighter and more percussive sound. Use an open palm and strike the strings with the inside of your fingers, avoiding your fingernails.

SLAP TAMBOUR

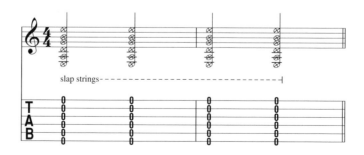

LESSON #62: LEFT-HAND FINGERING DECISIONS

You can play almost every pitch in multiple locations on the guitar fretboard. Deciding where to play a note affects the tone quality, articulation, and ease of playing. Let's use the beautiful Catalonian melody *El Noi De La Mare* as an example.

In this first example, the melody is played in the lowest position possible. The fingering is easy to read but requires a lot of shifting that disrupts the flow of the phrase.

EXAMPLE 1A

In this next example, the melody is played entirely in the fifth position. The notes are fretted higher on the fretboard and we can use vibrato to help shape the melody.

EXAMPLE 1B

Open Strings Can Help

Use an open string to help ease a position shift in fast scale passages:

EXAMPLE 2

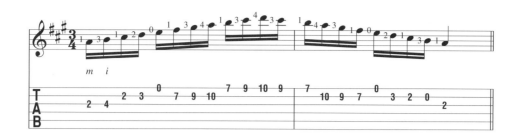

The example below is from the beautiful and virtuosic opening section of *Capricho àrabe* by Francisco Tàrrega (1852–1909). To play this piece, tune your sixth string down a whole step to D. In the third measure, use the open fourth string to facilitate the shift from seventh to first position.

EXAMPLE 3

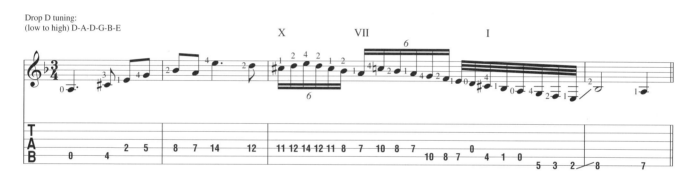

Campanella is the Italian word for "little bell." When applied to classical guitar fingering, it is the practice of playing stepwise notes on separate strings rather than fingering adjacent notes on the same string. The tones ring over each other, creating a beautiful and unique musical effect. The Spanish Renaissance composer Alonso Mudarra (1510–1580) features the campanella effect in his *Fantasia X*. Originally composed for the *vihuela*, a guitar-like Renaissance instrument, Mudarra includes the subtitle *Fantasía que contrahaze la harpa en la manera de Ludovico*. Fantasia imitates the harp of Ludovico, a famous Renaissance harpist. When you play the scale passage in measures 5–7 on multiple strings as indicated, the pitches of the scale ring over, imitating the sound of a harp.

EXAMPLE 4

No pain, no gain. That philosophy might work for exercise and athletics, but not for guitar playing. You should never feel pain during performance or practice. If you do, stop playing immediately and diagnose the problem. If you experience pain in your left hand, excessive pressure is often the cause.

Compare the width of your fingers to the width of the guitar strings. No competition, right? We can easily hold down the strings, yet in the heat of playing, we often use more left-hand pressure than is needed.

Sensitivity Exercise

In order to minimize the amount of pressure that we use, we first have to become aware of the problem. This exercise will help you to identify how much left-hand pressure is necessary to produce a pitch versus how much pressure you actually use.

Start by playing the note C on the third string, fifth fret. First, just place your left-hand finger on the string without any pressure. You should get a thud sound when you play. Slightly increase the pressure until you hear a buzz. Add just a tiny bit more pressure and you'll produce a clear tone.

Notice that there is a very small difference in left-hand pressure between producing a buzz and producing a clear pitch.

EXERCISE 1

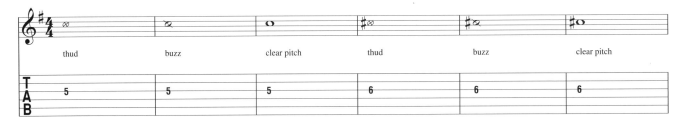

Now try this chromatic scale passage:

EXERCISE 2

Volume Does Matter

Often, we will unnecessarily use increased left-hand pressure to play loudly. Using more right-hand energy to produce louder notes can inadvertently influence the left hand and result in using additional pressure to fret a note. When this happens, try playing the passage very softly. Notice how your left hand relaxes the pressure. Slightly increase your playing volume while using minimum pressure with your left hand. Keep increasing the volume and energy in your right hand while using minimum pressure in your left.

Finger Distance Equals Increased Pressure

The further your fingers stretch to reach a chord, the more pressure you tend to use. Minimize your reach by practicing difficult chords and passages higher up the neck. Create an exercise in which you play the chord, release all pressure, then shift down a fret. The exercise will feel like you are bouncing down the fretboard. Apply minimum pressure as you play the chord, then relax immediately.

EXERCISE 3

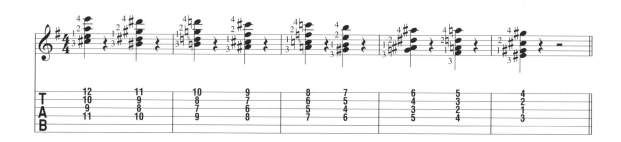

Guitar Setup and Action

Guitar action is the distance between the string and the fretboard. If the action is too low, the strings will buzz against the frets; too high an action, and it becomes difficult to fret the notes. To play with minimum left-hand pressure, make sure that your guitar is set up well. Play with the lowest action possible without the strings buzzing. A usual distance between the string and fingerboard is approximately 3.2 mm for the low E (sixth) string and 2.7 mm for the high E (first string) when measured at the 12th fret.

LESSON #64: NATURAL HARMONICS

Harmonics are high, chime-like sounds produced by touching the string at specific points along the fretboard. As a string vibrates, it creates a standing wave pattern. A *node* is a point along the vibrating string where the wave pattern seems to be standing still. Lightly touching the vibrating string at a node creates a harmonic.

Playing a harmonic at the 12th fret divides the vibrating string length in half and creates a harmonic one octave above the open string.

Touching the string at the seventh fret divides the vibrating string length into thirds and creates a harmonic an octave plus a 5th above the open string.

Touching the string at the fifth fret divides the vibrating string length into quarters and creates a harmonic two octaves above the open string.

As the chart below illustrates, additional harmonics can be produced. However, the lower on the neck you play a harmonic, the less accurate the pitch and more difficult it is to produce a tone.

Fret	Pitch Distance from Open String
12th	One octave
Seventh	One octave + 5th
Fifth	Two octaves
Fourth	Two octaves + major 3rd
Third	Two octaves + perfect 5th

The following harmonics are played at the 12th fret. Straighten your fourth finger and place it directly over the fret wire. Touch the strings lightly, without applying any pressure. You may find using the right side of the fourth finger works best, as it is bonier and has a harder surface. As you play each note, slightly lift your left hand finger from the string, and the sound will amplify.

EXAMPLE 1

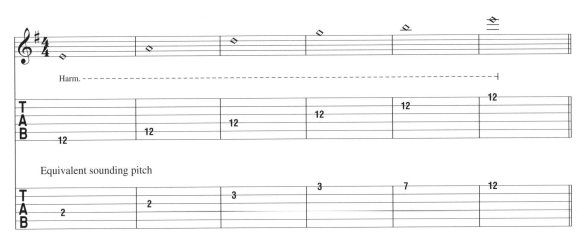

Play harmonics on the seventh fret with your first or second left-hand finger:

EXAMPLE 2

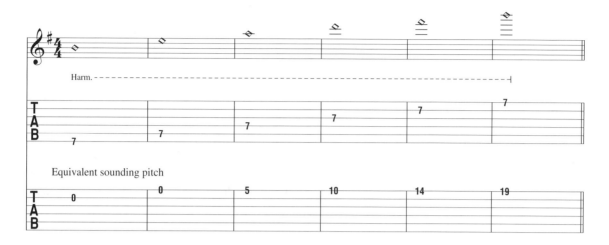

Fifth-fret harmonics are challenging to play clearly. Articulate the pitches with your right hand close to the bridge for increased volume.

EXAMPLE 3

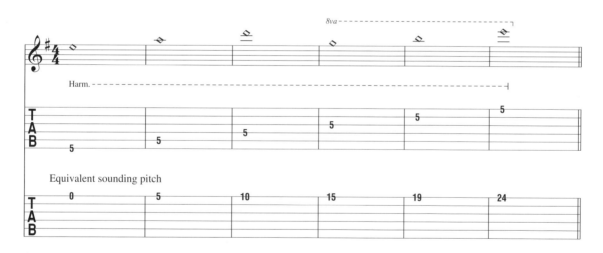

Playing effective harmonics is a study in opposites. Your left hand gently touches the string, using minimum pressure. To create volume and a clear pitch, your right hand plucks the string with good energy and speed.

LESSON #65: PIZZICATO

According to the *Harvard Dictionary of Music*, "pizzicato" is an indication that a note is to be plucked, rather than bowed. When playing guitar, all of the pitches are plucked, yet when pizzicato is indicated, we must change the tone quality so that the notes sound dry and muted.

To play a full pizzicato, damp the strings with your right-hand palm, just in front of the bridge. Rotate your arm to the right so that the side of your pinky lays across the six strings. Position your finger parallel to the bridge so that all the strings are muted evenly. On electric guitar, this technique is called *palm muting*.

Play with the flesh of your thumb, avoiding the fingernail. As you move from lower to higher strings, slide your palm towards the upper strings so that all pitches are evenly muted.

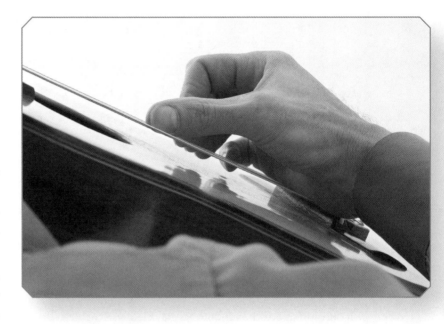

EXAMPLE 1

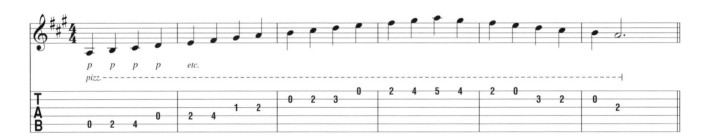

Use your thumb to play these triads pizzicato:

EXAMPLE 2

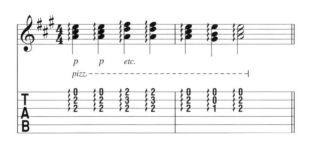

It's possible, but more difficult, to play pizzicato with your fingers. Adjust your right hand to make sure that you're damping all the strings that you play.

EXAMPLE 3

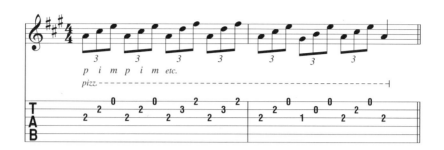

Some guitarists create pizzicato by playing with the flesh of the thumb, but not damping the strings with the right hand. This technique provides more overtones and volume than a palm mute and is still a contrast to a normally produced note.

EXAMPLE 4

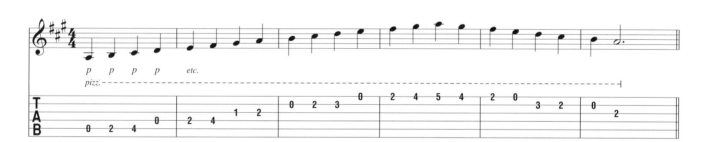

A more extreme and harsh-sounding technique is the *Bartók pizzicato*, or *snap pizzicato*.

Fret the note as normal. Hold the string between your right-hand thumb and index finger. Pull the string out and away from the fingerboard and then release it, allowing the string to snap against the frets.

EXAMPLE 5

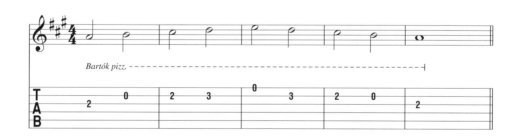

For an example of the Bartók pizzicato, listen to Leo Brouwer's ground-breaking guitar quartet "Cuban Landscape with Rain."

Playing above the 12th fret can be a daunting challenge. With the awkward position, high notes, and ledger lines, what's a guitarist to do?

Pitches and Notation

Notes on the 12th fret are one octave higher than the open string. Use the 12th fret for reference just as you would the open string in first position.

Although it's possible to play notes on the bass strings above the 12th fret, it's not very practical. Those pitches can be easily played in lower positions on higher strings. You will usually find notes on the third string up to the 15th fret, notes on the second string up to the 17th fret, and notes on the first string up to the 19th or 20th fret.

Twelfth position is made up of notes on frets 12 through 15 and includes the following natural pitches:

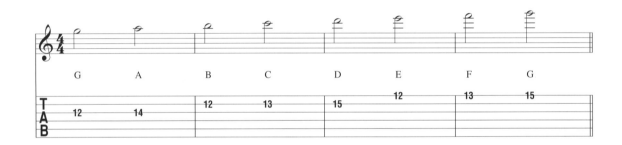

Think and say the note names as you play the following (semi) chromatic scale. Identify the notes by name, and you will soon become accustomed to reading the ledger lines.

Here's a (semi) chromatic scale in 12th position:

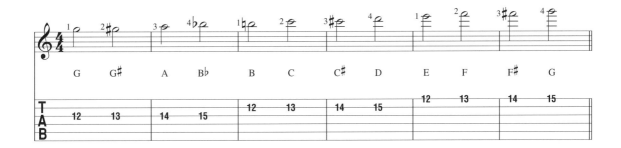

All classical guitars have 19 frets and can produce a high B on the first string. Depending on your luthier, you may have an instrument with an added 20th fret and can play a high C.

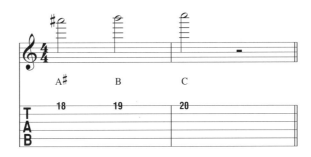

Playing Position

Some guitars have a cutaway or elevated fingerboard. This makes playing above the 12th fret easier. But even with a traditional classical guitar, it's possible to clearly play notes above the 12th fret.

Sitting in the traditional classical guitar position, bend from the waist and lower your shoulder. As you shift up to the 12th position, arch your wrist slightly and slide your left-hand thumb to the lower edge of the neck. Your thumb may rest directly behind the 12th fret as you play in the higher positions, or it can rest on the edge of the fretboard. For stability and accuracy, always keep your left-hand thumb in contact with the neck or fingerboard.

LESSON #67: RASGUEADO

Rasgueado is a percussive strumming technique popular in flamenco guitar styles and often used in classical guitar music, as well. To play a rasgueado, hit or strum the strings with the back of your fingers, striking your fingernails on the string.

Rasgueado patterns can be divided into two main categories: those that use individual finger movements and those that use rotation of the forearm to strike the strings.

Individual Finger Movement Patterns

Before playing rasgueado on the fingerboard, let's build up our strength and speed. Depending on the length of your thumb, either line up all your right-hand fingers on your thumb, if your thumb is long enough, or in the palm of your hand. Flick each finger off of you thumb or palm, creating a sound similar to a reverse snap. Keep a steady tempo, flicking each finger one at a time:

Index = *i*

Middle = *m*

Ring = *a*

Pinky = *c*

Once you can move your fingers independently, add resistance to your stroke. Place your hand on a table or other hard, flat surface and rhythmically flick your fingers. The back of your fingernails will hit and glide along the surface. Unless you don't mind scratching the finish, avoid practicing this on the back of your guitar.

Now you are ready to practice the rasgueado on the guitar. Damp the strings with your left hand as you play the following exercises. Set up your right hand so that the back of your fingernails will strike all six strings, lowest to highest, on the downstroke. On the upstroke, use the inside of your fingernail to strum the strings. You may miss playing the lowest bass strings when you execute the upstroke. You can rest your thumb lightly on the sixth string for stability, although doing this will omit the low E string from your strum.

The rasgueado is a very percussive technique. Move through the strings quickly, as if all six strings are played at once. Even though your movement is quick, practice the following patterns at a slow and even tempo before increasing the speed.

EXAMPLE 1

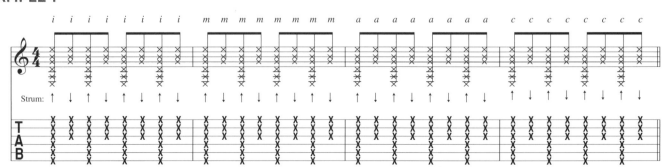

EXAMPLE 2

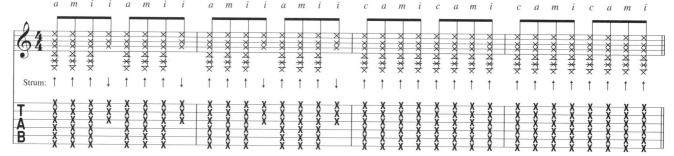

EXAMPLE 3

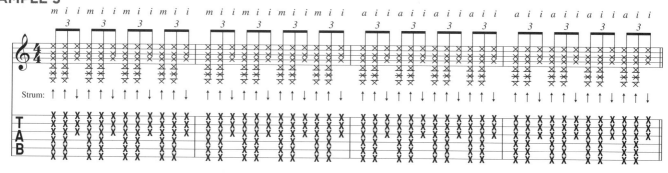

Patterns Using Arm Rotation

By rotating your forearm, you can play powerful rasgueado patterns that combine the fingers and thumb. The movement is like turning a door knob. Place your right hand near the strings so that your thumb is just below the first string. Play all six strings with a thumb upstroke by quickly rotating your forearm. Caution: you may strike and scratch the soundboard while using the stroke. This technique is best played on a guitar that has a tap plate or golpe plate to protect the wood.

EXAMPLE 4

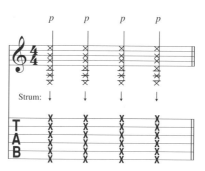

Now add a downstroke with the middle finger:

EXAMPLE 5

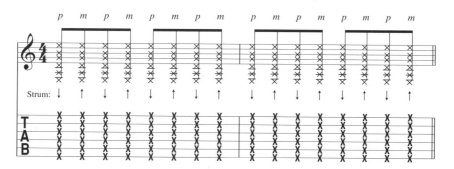

Here is an example of a triplet:

EXAMPLE 6

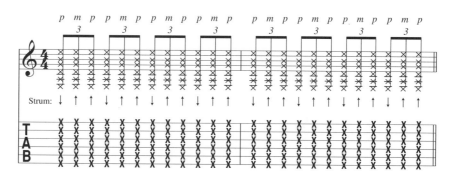

LESSON #68: REST STROKE SPEED EXERCISES

Rest stroke, or *supported stroke*, is the preferred right-hand method for articulating blazingly fast scales. After your finger plays a pitch, it rebounds off the lower adjacent string, which greatly helps with the velocity and volume of the stroke.

The quicker you can relax your finger, the faster you play. Hold your right hand out in front of you. Move your index finger toward your palm as if making a rest stroke. Make a small motion, covering only the distance that you would move when playing. Immediately relax your finger and return to your starting point. How fast can you return? The less time it takes for your finger to relax and return to the neutral starting part, the quicker you will be able to articulate notes on the guitar.

We all know the importance of alternating right-hand fingers, but the following exercise starts with a repeated finger workout. Relax the repeated finger completely before striking the next note. This is more of an exercise in quick relaxation than quick articulation.

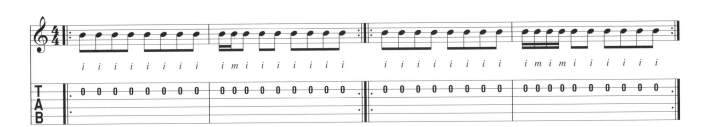

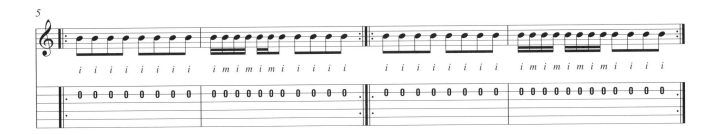

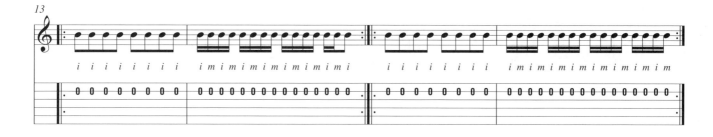

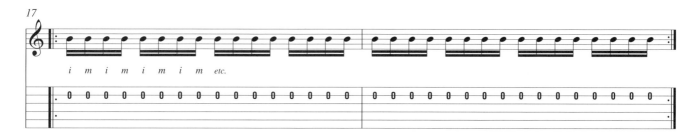

After practicing this exercise with index and middle fingers, try all the other finger combinations:

1. *m–i*

2. *i–a*

3. *a–i*

4. *m–a*

5. *a–m*

The first finger listed plays the repeated note in each measure. Both fingers alternate to articulate the faster-moving 16th notes.

Most players find the index/middle (*i–m*) and index/annular (*i–a*) finger combinations to be the quickest. Find your strongest combination and work towards maximum speed and volume.

Keep practicing the weaker finger combinations. With time and diligent practice, these combinations will improve, as well.

LESSON #69: RIGHT-HAND FINGERING CONSIDERATIONS

From the first day of studying classical guitar, we learn the importance of always alternating our right-hand fingers. However, there are more options to consider than just strict alternation.

Most editions of classical guitar music include extensive suggestions for left-hand fingerings. Far fewer include right-hand fingering recommendations. Often, students come to their lesson complaining about a difficult section of a piece, even after many hours of practicing. They've carefully decided on their left-hand fingering, notating it in the music when necessary, yet they have not paid attention to how they will play the passage with their right hand. We might think that letting the right hand do *whatever is comfortable* is enough. In my experience, this leads to uneasiness in performance and mistakes under pressure.

String Crossing

When changing strings in a melody or arpeggio, cross up with a higher finger and down with a lower finger. For example, when moving from the third string (G) to the second string (B), use any of the following fingerings:

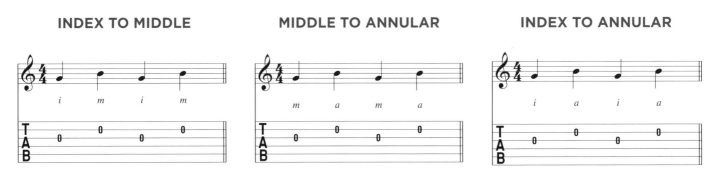

Use the opposite fingerings when crossing from the second string (B) to the third string (G):

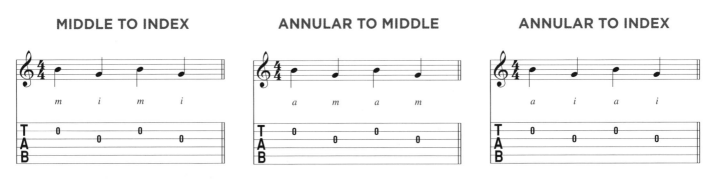

Skip a String, Skip a Finger

You can use adjacent or non-adjacent fingers to play neighboring strings. However, when playing two notes on non-adjacent strings, either in a chord, arpeggio, or melody, always skip a finger.

EXAMPLE 1

Your Thumb Is a Finger, Too

Although the thumb is used most often to play the bass strings, you can also use it to play the treble strings to help facilitate right-hand fingerings.

EXAMPLE 2

Yes, Virginia, It's OK to Repeat a Finger

If all classical guitar repertoire was written on a single string, we could alternate our right-hand fingers 100 percent of the time. To preserve optimal right-hand fingering, avoid awkward string crossings and accommodate variable right-hand string spacing. It is occasionally necessary to repeat a finger. If possible, repeat a finger after a relatively long note, at the beginning of a new phrase, or after a slur.

Don't Leave It to Chance

Pay attention to your right-hand fingering. Take time to decide which fingering works best for you and practice/play the passage with the same fingering every time. Under pressure of performance, you'll be calm and confident knowing your right-hand fingering is reliable and effective.

LESSON #70: SPEED BURSTS

To play fast, we have to practice fast. Speed-burst practice on short musical fragments increases speed without sacrificing accuracy.

Let's start by building right-hand articulation speed. Play each measure as quickly and loudly as possible. Relax as you play the long note. Immediate and complete relaxation is the key to playing fast. Don't leave any tension in your hands. Complete relaxation prepares your finger to play the next note. The quicker you completely relax, the quicker you play the next note.

EXERCISE 1

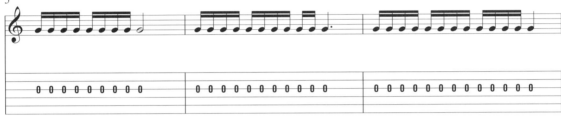

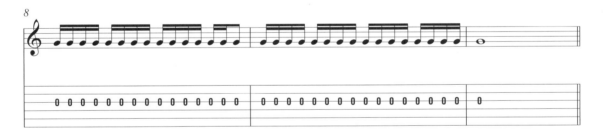

Now add the left-hand fingering and work speed bursts with the G major scale. Completely relax your left and right hands as you play the long note. The relaxed weight of your left-hand finger is sufficient to keep the long note ringing. No need to press; just relax as the long note rings.

EXERCISE 2

Whenever you encounter a hard shift or difficult transition, identify the problem spot and practice by using speed bursts.

The following A minor scale includes a shift from second to fifth position as you move from B to C.

EXERCISE 3

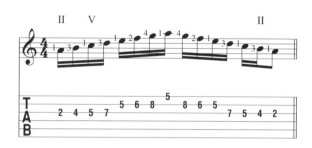

Isolate the shift and create a speed-burst exercise.

Work the ascending shift:

EXERCISE 3A

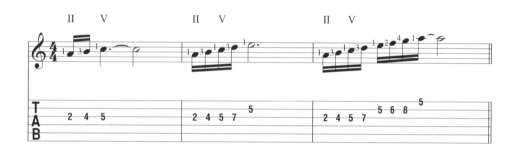

Work the descending shift:

EXERCISE 3B

Then put the scale together:

EXERCISE 3C

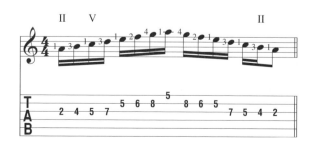

LESSON #71: TONE COLOR

The classical guitar isn't the loudest instrument, but what it lacks in volume, it makes up for in variety of tone color. Changing the location where you pluck the string will change the timbre of the sound.

Natural Sound

Most guitarists produce a natural, or normal, sound by plucking the string at the outer edge or just below the rosette. Rest stroke and free stroke are used to create a strong, full-bodied tone.

Ponticello/Metallic

Ponticello is the Italian word for "bridge." Playing the string near the bridge produces a bright or metallic sound. The closer to the bridge you play, the more strident and metallic the tone.

To play ponticello, start in your natural playing position, open up your elbow, and slide your right forearm slightly closer to the bridge. Your hand will drop toward the bridge and your fingers will cross the strings at a more perpendicular angle.

EXAMPLE 1

Composers may notate in the score *ponticello*, *sul ponticello* (on the bridge), or *metallico*. Even if not specifically notated, you can use ponticello to create contrast in a repeated section, mark a sharp accent, or help add volume to a crescendo.

In the excerpt below, from the famous *Canarios* by Gaspar Sanz, the melody repeats at measure 5. Play the repeated section ponticello. The contrast in tone color will add interest.

EXAMPLE 2

Tasto

The markings *tasto* and *sul tasto* are an instruction to pluck the string with your hand over the fretboard. This creates a darker, gentler, and sweeter sound. In guitar music, it is sometimes called a *dolce*.

To play *tasto*, start in your natural playing position, close your elbow just a little, and slide your right forearm slightly closer to the fretboard. Your hand will hover over the 15th–19th frets. By hovering over the frets, you will have less room to push the string down to prepare your stroke, thereby producing a softer sound.

EXAMPLE 3

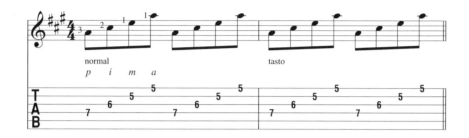

Changing the timbre of your sound adds another dimension to your performance. Composers rarely mark tone-color changes in the score. Experiment with changing the tone color and increase the expressiveness in your performances.

LESSON #72: TREMOLO

Tremolo is one of the most beautiful and evocative techniques used in classical guitar music. Repeating the same note at a fast tempo, tremolo creates the illusion of a sustained pitch.

Some of the most famous pieces in the classical guitar repertoire that use the tremolo technique are:

- *Recuerdos de la Alhambra* by Francisco Tárrega
- *Una Limosna por el Amor de Dios* by Agustín Barrios Mangoré
- *Campanas del Alba* by Eduardo Sainz de la Maza

Tremolo consists of the thumb playing a bass line followed by four or five repetitions of a treble note. The most common classical guitar tremolo fingering is *p–a–m–i*. Flamenco guitarists play a five-note tremolo: *p–i–a–m–i*.

Start your tremolo practice by placing all of your fingers (*p–i–m–a*) on the second string (B). Make sure that your thumb is in front of your fingers so that it will clear the index finger when you complete the thumb stroke and follow through.

Align your hand so that your large knuckles (metacarpophalangeal joints) hover directly above the second string (i.e., the string you are playing). This position may be different from what you are used to; your wrist may be a little higher than normal. Your fingers will come across the string at just about a right angle, and that's a great position at which to start practicing your tremolo.

Ultimately, we are aiming for a fast, even tremolo with good volume. To accomplish this, start practicing your tremolo slowly and loudly. Use a metronome to keep your tempo even, and play with strong, deliberate free strokes.

Believe it or not, the most effective way to develop a smooth and *legato* tremolo is to practice *staccato*. Play the following exercise by placing each finger on the string early, which will cut off the previous note. This will train your fingers to recover immediately. You will get to the next note quickly even though you are practicing slowly.

EXERCISE 1

EXERCISE 2

Alternate your thumb between two different strings and this exercise becomes more difficult. Notice that the first and last note of the tremolo will no longer sound staccato. Focus on returning your fingers to the string as early as possible.

EXERCISE 3

Thumb and finger independence is essential for an effective tremolo. As you play different bass notes with your thumb, keep your palm stable and your fingers hovering over the second string.

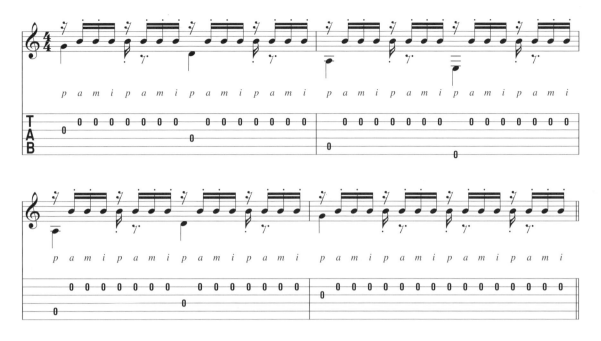

When you are ready to build up speed, use speed bursts to practice each of the previous exercises.

EXERCISE 4

EXERCISE 5

Practicing your tremolo on the second string (B) is more difficult than playing it on the first string. Playing on an inner string requires you to minimize excess finger motion and increase your accuracy. Once you master playing the tremolo on the second string, playing on the first string will be a breeze.

LESSON #73: TRILLS

The *trill* is a common ornament used in Baroque music in which the main note rapidly alternates with an upper auxiliary note (i.e., the scale tone directly above the main note). Baroque trills are played on the beat and most often start with the upper note. The upper auxiliary is a non-chord tone. Starting the trill on this dissonant pitch adds harmonic interest to the piece.

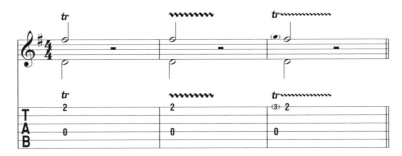

The three symbols above all indicate the occurrence of a trill. Even when a trill is not indicated in the score, if stylistically correct, the ornament may be added. The number of alternations between the two notes is variable. The trill can continue for the entire duration of the note or end early. The upper note is a non-chord tone that creates stress and harmonic interest. An upper-note trill may start with a long first note, stressing the dissonance of the non-chord tone. Here are a few examples:

EXAMPLE 1

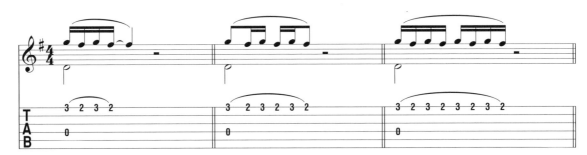

Single-String Trills

Trills are performed with a single articulation of the first note. All of the following notes are slurred. Practice playing the following trill. Start with both your first and second fingers on the string. Play G as normal. Pull off with the second finger to play the F#, then hammer on to play the G. Repeat.

EXAMPLE 2

You may find that alternating your left-hand fingers produces a more even and faster trill.

EXAMPLE 3

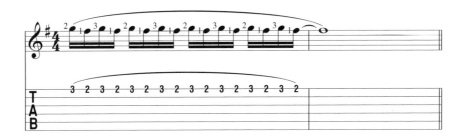

Here is an example of a trill in context:

"Sarabande" from *Cello Suite No. 1, BWV 1007* by J.S. Bach (1685–1750)

EXAMPLE 4

Drop D tuning:
(low to high) D-A-D-G-B-E

Cross-String Trills

In certain situations, you can play a trill on two adjacent strings. Play the following exercise slowly. Be sure to precisely follow the right-hand fingering.

EXAMPLE 5

Once you can play the preceding cross-string example slowly and evenly, try playing some short trills at tempo.

EXAMPLE 6

EXAMPLE 7

Upon completion of the cross-string trill, return your *annular* finger (*a*, or ring finger) to the higher string to damp the upper auxiliary note.

Often you will have the option to play trills on a single string or cross string. Context and personal taste will help you decide which works best.

Here is the opening from "Sarabande," *Lute Suite 1, BWV 996*, by J.S. Bach. Try playing the trill cross-string and on a single string.

EXAMPLE 8A

EXAMPLE 8B

LESSON #74: VIBRATO

According to the *New Harvard Dictionary of Music*, *vibrato* is a "slight fluctuation of pitch used by performers to enrich or intensify the sound." To create vibrato on the classical guitar, move the string laterally, from side to side, pulling the pitch slightly out of tune and then back.

Start by playing the note B on the seventh fret, sixth string with your second finger. Keeping your fingertip in the same place on the string, rotate the pressure on the string toward the bridge, back to neutral (N), then toward the headstock. As you push toward the bridge, the pitch goes slightly flat; as you pull toward the headstock, the pitch moves slightly sharp.

Keep your wrist straight and steady as you play. The motion begins in the elbow and moves the forearm side to side. Your left-hand thumb can remain on the back of the neck or it can be lifted away from the guitar. Some guitarists find that they can get a wider amplitude of motion with the thumb off the neck.

Set your metronome to 70 bpm or lower and play the following exercise. Stay relaxed. If tension starts to creep in, stop, take a breath, and start over.

*Push toward the bridge, pitch goes flat. Pull toward the headstock, pitch goes sharp.

Next, practice the exercise using the first, third, and fourth fingers. When you feel comfortable and relaxed playing at this tempo, slightly increase metronome speed. Aim for an ultimate speed of 90 bpm.

Vibrato on the guitar is played much slower than on the violin. If you vibrate too fast, the guitar sounds choked up and nervous.

Practice the previous exercise on all strings and all notes from fret 5 to fret 11.

Experiment with different methods to play your vibrato:

1. Start with a straight tone, then add vibrato.

2. Begin your vibrato before you articulate the sound.

3. Start with a slow vibrato and then speed up.

4. Start with a fast vibrato and then slow down.

Lateral, or side-to-side, vibrato as described above works best between the fifth and 12th frets. Below the fifth fret, the vibrating string is too long for our vibrato to affect any real change in the intonation.

Use vibrato as an ornament and add it to long notes in expressive lines. Unlike a violinist or cellist, guitarists add vibrato sparingly. It's a wonderful ornament to use, but it's not practical to vibrate on all the notes that we play.

LESSON #75: "LARGO" FROM CONCERTO IN D (VIVALDI)

The Baroque composer Antonio Vivaldi originally wrote the *Concerto in D, RV 93* for solo lute, accompanied by two violins and cello. Like most Baroque chamber concertos, this work is in three movements and follows the usual pattern: fast, slow, fast (or allegro, largo, allegro). This beautiful piece translates easily to guitar and is a staple of the classical guitar literature.

In order to perform the beautiful second movement of this concerto, we need to familiarize ourselves with an important aspect of Baroque performance: ornamentation. *Ornamentation* can be divided into two basic categories:

1. Ornamental figures that are added to individual notes. These may be indicated in the score or added by the performer.

2. *Free ornamentation*, or the recomposing/ornamentation of a melodic line. This is often performed on the repeat of a section and to fill in a long pause or major cadence.

Baroque ornamentation provides freedom for the performer, as no two performances of the same piece will be exactly alike.

The following is an ornamented example of the first part, or A section, of Vivaldi's *Concerto in D, RV93, Largo*. The top score reflects the music as originally written. The bottom score illustrates an ornamented version of the piece.

Baroque ornamental figures begin on the beat and are designed to create both harmonic and melodic interest. The ornamental figures added in this example are all played on one string and articulated with a slur. Specific ornamental figures added to the score include the following:

▶ An *appoggiatura* is a non-chord tone that is played on the beat and resolves by a whole step, usually in a downward motion (measure 1, beat 3: F♯–E).

▶ The Baroque *trill*, like an appoggiatura, starts most often with the upper note and resolves down by a whole step. Alternate between these two notes as many times as desired. Complete the trill on the main note (measure 4, beat 4: B–A–B–A; measure 8, beat 2: C♯–B–C♯–B).

▶ The *turn*, or cadence, starts with the upper note, plays the main note, descends to the lower neighbor note, and returns to the main note (measure 7, beat 3: B–A–G♯–A).

Free ornamentation is present throughout the ornamented version. Notice that the newly composed lines use scale-like motion and interval leaps but always remain within the harmonic structure of the piece.

Practice the original and ornamented examples below. Then work out your own ornamented performance.

 ORIGINAL

 **ORNAMENTED**

CONCERTO IN D, LARGO

Antonio Vivaldi

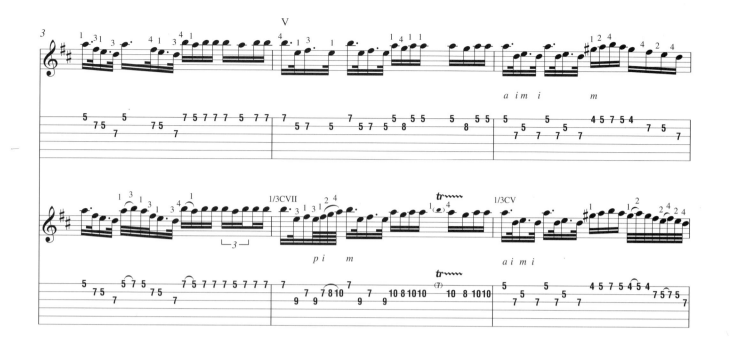

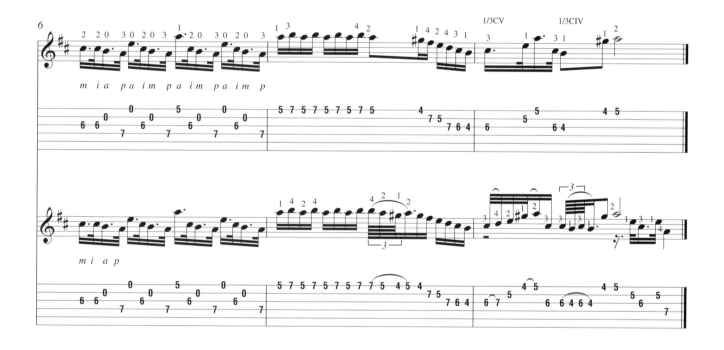

LESSON #76: WARMUP EXERCISES

Including a short warmup session (5–10 minutes) in each practice session will do more than just loosen up your hands; it will prevent future injuries and help you build a healthy and effective playing technique.

Warm up with a set of easy and basic movements, starting at a slow tempo. Play your warmup exercises with the best tone possible. Remember how it feels to play with a relaxed and efficient technique. You may play at a slower speed during your warmup, but strive to reproduce the same tone and finger accuracy that you achieved at the end of your last practice session.

The following chart contains all the possible left-hand finger patterns available that use each finger only once. Since frets on the guitar are wider as you approach the lower position, we will begin the exercise at the ninth position. As you shift lower on the neck, the guitar will gently challenge your left hand to stretch a little farther.

1 2 3 4	2 1 3 4	3 1 2 4	4 1 2 3
1 2 4 3	2 1 4 3	3 1 4 2	4 1 3 2
1 3 2 4	2 3 1 4	3 2 1 4	4 2 1 3
1 3 4 2	2 3 4 1	3 1 2 4	4 2 3 1
1 4 3 2	2 4 1 3	3 4 1 2	4 3 1 2
1 4 2 3	2 4 3 1	3 4 2 1	4 3 2 1

EXERCISE 1

Play one pattern on all six strings, starting with the high E string and moving to the lowest string. Keep lower left-hand fingers on the fretboard whenever possible.

Complete the exercise in ninth position, then shift down to eighth position and play the same pattern, ascending from the sixth to first string. Continue playing the same pattern in all positions.

Use the following right-hand fingerings:

▶ *i–m*

▶ *m–i*

▶ *i–a*

▶ *a–i*

▶ *a–m*

▶ *m–a*

▶ *i–m–a–m*

▶ *a–m–i–m*

Practice the exercise with free stroke and rest stroke.

Play slowly with a consistent tempo, great tone, and minimum left-hand movement.

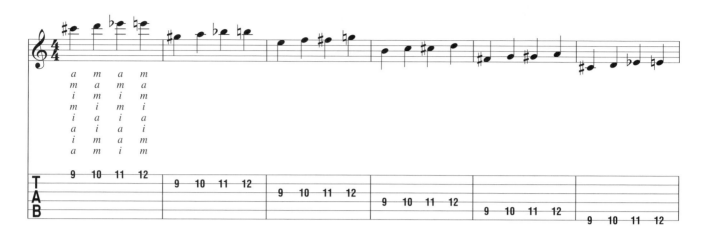

EXERCISE 2

Use the previous Exercise 1 for this exercise, but this time, repeat each pitch four times, like you are playing 16th notes.

Try these right-hand fingerings:

- *i–m–i–m*
- *m–i–m–i*
- *i–a–i–a*
- *a–i–a–i*
- *i–m–a–m*
- *a–m–i–m*
- *p–a–m–i* (the tremolo fingering)

Practice a few of the finger combinations every day. Some of the patterns will be more challenging for you than others. Make a note of which ones are the most difficult and focus your practice on the more challenging combinations.

LESSON #77: VALSE, OP. 7, NO. 1 (AGUADO)

Composed by one of the great classical-era guitarists, Dionisio Aguado (1784–1849), this *Valse* is the first in a collection of four valse faciles. Although not as easy as the title would suggest, don't let the E major key signature, with its four sharps, dissuade you from playing this lovely piece.

▶ **Measure 14, beat 3:** play E♯

▶ **Measure 15:** play E natural

▶ **Measure 16, beat 2:** The "X" before the note C indicates a double sharp. The pitches are written as C double sharp and E♯.

Which sounds the same as D and F.

▶ **Measure 24:** Playing the B open may seem unconventional, but it makes for a very comfortable left-hand fingering. Slide your third finger from the D♯ on the fifth string up one fret to the E for a smooth transition.

▶ **Measure 25:** The key modulates to A major. D is now natural, except where marked with an accidental.

▶ **Measure 32:** Maintain left-hand pressure while you slide the second and third fingers up one fret to create a double slur.

▶ **Measures 34–36:** This left-hand fingering sustains the dotted quarter notes in the bass while the upper voice moves from D♯ to E.

VALSE, OP. 7, NO. 1

Dionisio Aguado

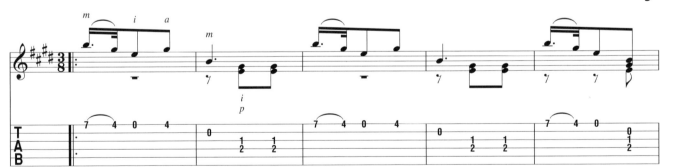

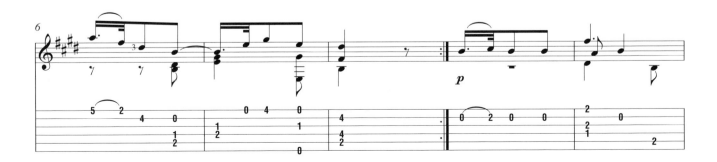

The Spanish guitarist and composer Dionisio Aguado (1784–1849) composed grand concert works, etudes, and charming short pieces for guitar. His method book, *Escuela de Guitarra*, published in 1825, was the first tutor to recommend using fingernails to stroke the strings.

This piece comes from a collection of 12 Valses, *Douze Valses pour Guitare Seule, Oeuv 1*, published by B. Schott.

Don't let the brevity of this piece fool you—this Valse is a fun piece to play and hear.

The Valse is written in 3/8, although each measure should be felt as one large beat. The last eighth note of each measure often serves as a pickup to the next beat.

▶ **Measure 15:** Slide your first finger along the first string to connect F and B.

▶ **Measure 16:** Slide your fourth finger along the first string to connect G and C.

▶ **Measure 17:** The entire measure can be played in first position but, to better bring out the motif, fret the F on the second string, sixth fret. Slide your fourth finger along the second string to connect D and F.

Observe the first and second endings the first time through the piece. Take the *Da Capo* return to the beginning of the piece. This time, though, only play the second ending. End the piece in measure 18 (at the *Fine*).

VALSE, OP. 1, NO. 2

Dionisio Aguado

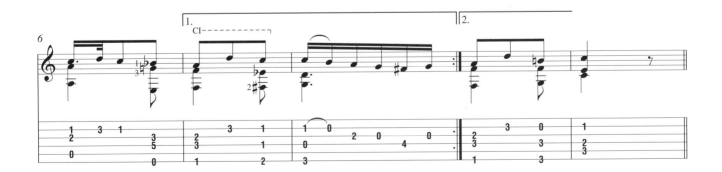

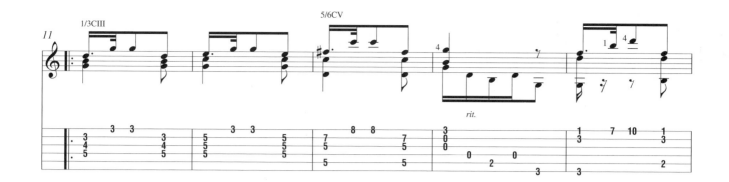

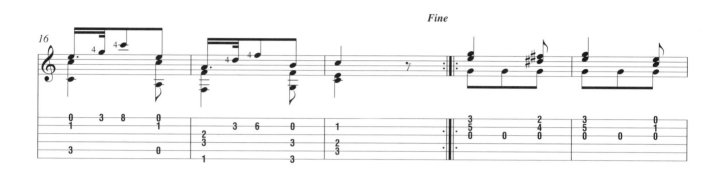

LESSON #79: ALTERNATE TUNINGS

A majority of classical guitar repertoire uses standard tuning. In a few cases, composers will require the guitarist to change the tuning of one, two, or more strings. This increases the range of the guitar, eases fingering difficulties, and allows the composer to explore different sonorities.

Two guitar-like instruments were popular during the Renaissance era: the Renaissance *lute* and *vihuela*. The lute was popular throughout Europe. The vihuela was played in Spain, Italy, and Portugal. The intervallic tuning of both of these instruments is similar to our modern-day guitar, with the third string tuned down one half step.

LUTE/VIHUELA TUNING

John Dowland (1563–1636), the English Renaissance lutenist and composer, was the most famous musician of his time. Play this excerpt from Dowland's solo lute work "Come Away" with the third string tuned down to F#:

EXAMPLE 1

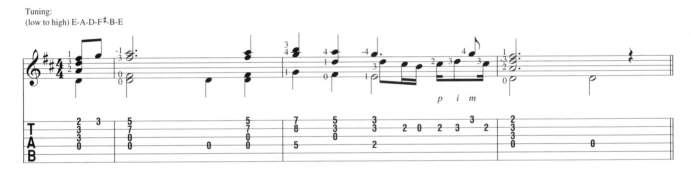

Tuning the sixth string down a whole step from E to D (drop D tuning) increases the lower range of the guitar and is especially well-suited for pieces written in the key of D.

In one of the major Classical era works written for guitar, *Grand Solo, Op. 14*, composer and guitarist Fernando Sor (1778–1839) begins the composition with a low, open D string pedal tone. During the fourth measure of the open D pedal tone, Sor breaks the pattern and writes an ascending bass line rising from the low D.

EXAMPLE 2

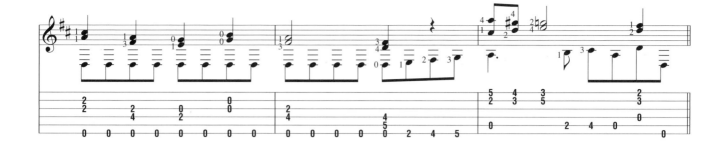

Additional Alternate Tunings

The great Paraguayan classical guitarist/composer Agustín Barrios Mangoré (1855–1944) wrote beautiful compositions requiring the fifth string, A, to be tuned down a whole step to G, and the sixth string, E, tuned down a whole step to D:

▶ "Chôro da Saudade"

▶ "Un Sueño en la Floresta"

▶ "Caazapà-Aire Popular Paraguayo"

BARRIOS TUNING

 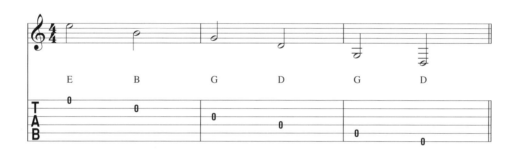

American guitarist/composer Andrew York's famous piece "Sunburst" is played with both the first and sixth strings tuned down a whole step from E to D (double drop D tuning).

DOUBLE DROP D TUNING

 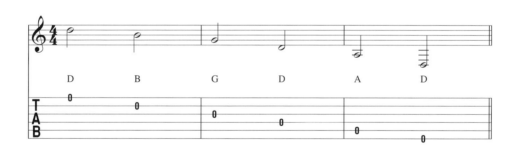

In his four-movement suite for guitar, *Koyunbaba, (Op. 19)* Carlo Domeniconi (b. 1947) uses open D minor tuning:

OPEN D MINOR TUNING

 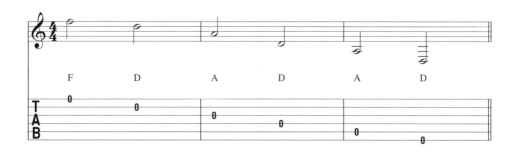

LESSON #80: ARTICULATIONS

The guitar won't win any awards for being the loudest instrument, but it may be one of the most expressive. Our instrument's expressive nature is in part due to the variety of articulations available to the skilled guitarist.

Legato

The Italian term *legato* indicates to play a selection smoothly and connected, without observable space between successive notes. This is the default articulation that we strive for, yet it is difficult to create. Pay attention to the end of each note so that you can smoothly connect it to the beginning of the next pitch. Matching the volume, tone color, and duration of successive notes helps create the illusion of a connected line.

Playing a slur takes legato to the next level. *Slurs* are notated as a curved line that connects two or more notes and instructs the musician to play all the notes under the slur marking with one articulation. To play a slur on the guitar, pluck the first note, then use only the left hand to articulate the notes under the slur marking. An ascending slur is played by *hammering onto* the next higher pitch. A descending slur is played by *pulling off* to the next, lower pitch. Because only the first note of a slur is articulated with the right hand, the pitches are played legato, with the first note of the slur sounding the loudest.

EXAMPLE 1

Staccato

Staccato is the opposite of legato. Staccato notes are marked by a dot above or below the notehead and are played with an obvious break between pitches. To create staccato articulation, place your right-hand finger on the ringing strings, dampening the sound.

It's easiest to articulate single-note staccato lines if all the pitches are on the same string. By anticipating the placement of your right-hand finger on the string, you will cut off the previously sounding notes.

EXAMPLE 2

Study No. 20, Op. 31 (Sor/Segovia Study 9) by Fernando Sor (1778–1839) is an excellent staccato workout. Bring your right-hand fingers to the strings immediately after playing each chord.

EXAMPLE 3

Lifting left-hand pressure helps create the staccato. However, if you release the left-hand pressure without damping with the right hand, you'll create extraneous noises similar to a descending slur.

Accent

An *accent* is the indication to play a specific note or chord loudly, followed by an immediate decline in volume. Different than the dynamic marking *forte,* or loud, the accent is applied to only a single note or chord.

The following symbols all indicate an accent:

*forte/piano   **sforzando

Roll

Playing a chord with five or six strings requires a roll; however, you can also roll a four-note chord, three-note triad, or two-note dyad. Execute the roll using all thumb, or with a combination of thumb and fingers.

EXAMPLE 4

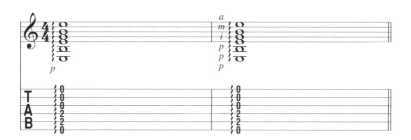

Choose how fast or slow to play your roll and whether to start the first note of the roll (usually the bass) or the last note of the roll (usually the highest note of the chord) on the beat.

"Sarabande," from *Cello Suite No. 1, BWV 1007* by J.S. Bach, begins with a rolled D major chord followed by G major. Start the rolls slightly ahead of the beat and articulate the last note of each roll on the beat. This will establish a steady pulse and highlight the melody notes.

EXAMPLE 5

LESSON #81: BACH AND THE GUITAR

Johann Sebastian Bach (1685–1750), arguably the greatest composer of all time, never wrote for guitar, yet his compositions are a major part of the classical guitar repertoire.

An inventory of Bach's estate after his death identifies two keyboard instruments that were strung with gut strings and that imitated the sound of a lute. These instruments, called "Lautenwerk," or lute-harpsichord, may have been the instrument that Bach used to compose his lute suites. Whether Bach intended his suites to be played on such a keyboard instrument or on the lute is a subject for debate. However, the proof of such an instrument in Bach's collection led lutenists, and later, guitarists to adopt this repertoire as their own.

The letters BWV always accompany the title of Bach's music. "BWV" is the abbreviation for *Bach-Werke-Verzeichnis*, a systematic thematic catalogue of the musical works of J.S. Bach. This collection of the complete works by Bach was edited by Wolfgang Schmieder. Schmieder organized Bach's music by genre, not by date. While the BWV letters accurately identify every piece that Bach composed, they do not indicate the date or chronological order of his compositions.

Unaccompanied Music for Violin, Cello, and Lute

Bach's solo instrumental works include three sonatas and three partitas for solo violin (BWV 1001–1006) and six cello suites (BWV 1007–1012).

He composed four lute suites (BWV 995–997, 1000, and 1006a), as well as the *Prelude, Fugue, and Allegro* (BWV 998), and *Little Prelude for Lute* (BWV 999). *Fugue for Lute* (BWV 1000) is a transcription of this same work for violin (BWV 1001). The lute version was transcribed by Johann Christian Weyrauch, a contemporary of Bach.

The Baroque suite, or partita, is a collection of dance music in which all the movements share the same key. Bach's solo instrumental suites and partitas include stylized dance movements, which are artistic interpretations of dance forms, and not necessarily meant to accompany dance.

Bach Transcribing Bach

Bach frequently reused or recycled his motifs and musical materials. *Lute Suite III, BWV 995* is Bach's own reworking of his *Cello Suite, BWV 1011*. Below is an excerpt of *Gavotte I*. Bach's version for cello is written in C minor and placed underneath the guitar version for comparison. His lute version, although originally written in G minor, is most often played on guitar in A minor, as reflected in this score. Arranging his cello work for lute, Bach added bass lines and rearranged the chord voicings as needed.

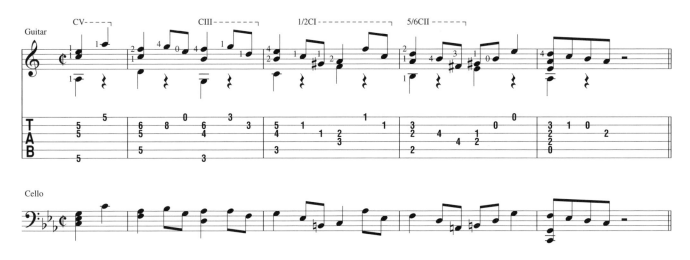

Similarly, *Lute Suite IV, BWV 1006a* is Bach's reworking of his *Violin Partita III, BWV 1006*.

Following Bach's example of transcribing violin and cello music for the lute, guitarists enjoy playing Bach's *Lute Suites*, as well as transcriptions of the cello suites and violin partitas and sonatas.

Works for Lute by J.S. Bach

▶ *BWV 995, originally in G minor (III), based on* Cello Suite V

    Prelude

    Allemande

    Courante

    Sarabande

    Gavotte I and II

    Gigue

▶ *BWV 996, originally in E minor (I)*

    Prelude/Presto

    Allemande

    Courante

    Sarabande

    Bourrée

    Giga

▶ *BWV 997, originally in C minor (II)*

    Praeludio

    Fuga

    Sarabande

    Gigue

    Double

▶ *BWV 998, Prelude, Fugue, and Allegro*

▶ *BWV 999, Prelude in C minor*

▶ *BWV 1000, Fuga, based on BWV 1001, Violin Sonata*

▶ *BWV 1006a, originally in E major (IV), based on Violin Partita III*

    Prelude

    Loure

    Gavotte en Rondeau

    Minuet I and II

    Bourrée

    Gigue

Matteo Carcassi (1792–1853), an Italian-born guitarist and pianist, was active as a teacher and performer in Paris. His *25 Etudes Melodious*, published in 1825, are still a staple of the classical guitar repertoire.

Etude 3 is a study in non-chord tones. Each measure consists of a single harmony. The melodic note on beat 2 is a non-chord, or dissonant, note that resolves downward by a whole or half step on beat 3.

Measure 1 consists of an A major chord. F♯ is a dissonant non-chord tone that resolves down by a whole step to E. Measure 2 begins with an E7 chord. The F♯ is a dissonant non-chord tone that resolves to E, and the pattern continues throughout the piece. Highlight the motion of the dissonant non-chord tone resolving downward by a whole or half step: stress the dissonant note played on beat 2 with a louder articulation, then relax the volume as the motif resolves downward on beat 3.

Practice the harmonic reduction of measures 1–4. Bring out the melody and dynamic shape of each measure.

EXAMPLE 1

As you play the written arpeggio, bring out the melody with rest strokes, and inflect each non-chord-tone-to-chord-tone motif with the appropriate dynamic shape.

ETUDE 3

Matteo Carcassi

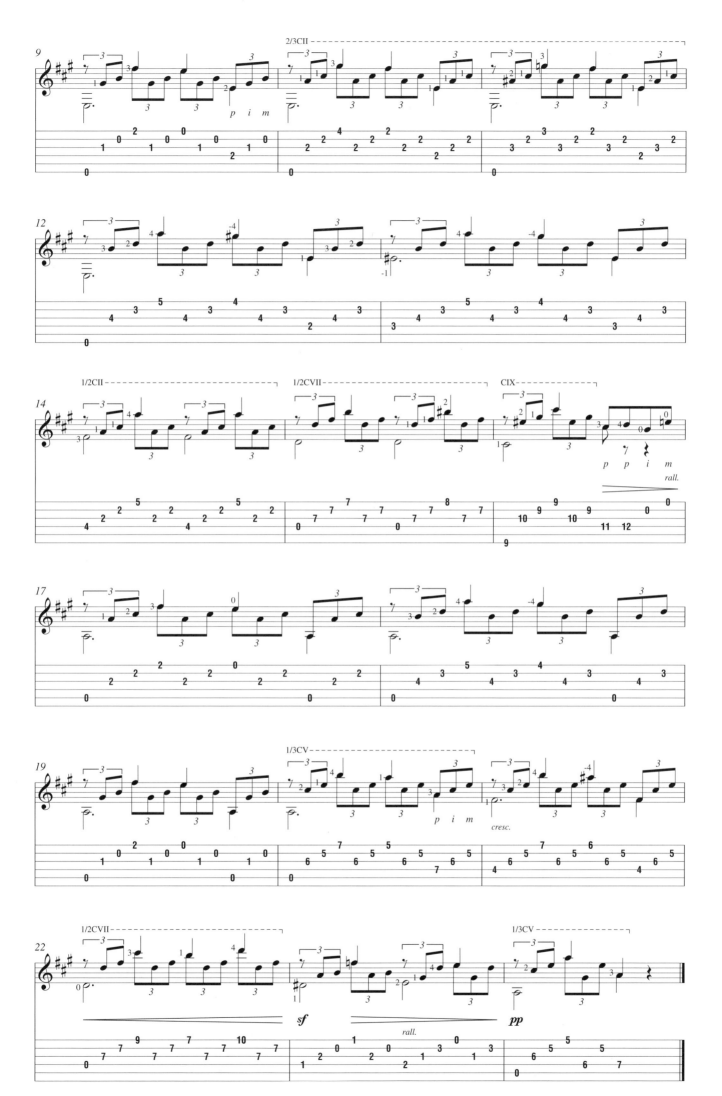

LESSON #83: WALTZ, OP. 27 (CARULLI)

Although this Carulli piece was printed without any dynamic or tone color markings, use dynamics to inflect the four-bar phrases, and tone-color changes to create interest on the repeats.

WALTZ, OP. 27

Ferdinand Carulli

Tuning the sixth string down a whole step from E to D increases the lower range of the guitar. This tuning is especially well-suited for pieces written in the key of D, in which you can add the open D pedal tone. The notes played on the sixth string are written at pitch:

DROP D TUNING

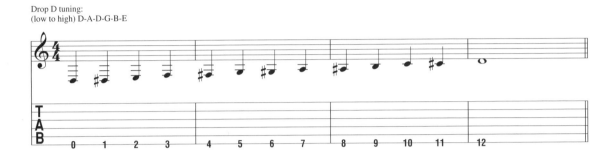

The theme of Fernando Sor's *Introduction and Variations on the Malbroug Aria, Op. 28* is an excellent example of the open sixth-string D used as a pedal tone.

▶ In measures 16–17, use your second finger as a guide finger, sliding between the D and C♯.

▶ In measures 17–18, use your first finger as a guide finger, sliding between the D and C.

▶ In measure 19, the left-hand fingering is a little awkward. Use your first finger on the G so that the pitch can sustain as you play the B and D and, if possible, connect to the F♯ on the following beat.

INTRODUCTION AND VARIATIONS ON THE MALBROUG ARIA, OP. 28

Fernando Sor

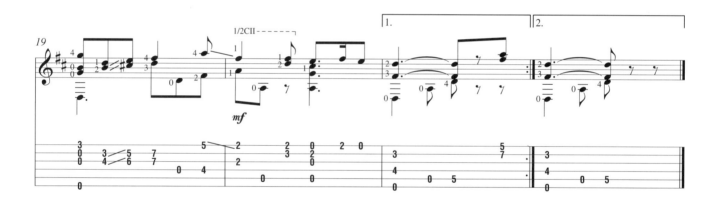

LESSON #85: GUITAR CARE AND MAINTENANCE

Whether you've invested your life savings or just a few dollars into a classical guitar, your instrument needs proper care to remain in good playing condition.

Environment

Humidity and temperature are two variables that greatly affect all wood instruments. Solid wood guitars should ideally be stored in 50-percent humidity. Depending on the season and climate, you may be battling to keep a dry guitar humidified or to dry out an over-humidified instrument.

Dry Climate and Cold Temperature

Run your fingers along the side of the neck. Sharp fret wires protruding over the side of the fretboard indicate that your guitar is too dry. The wooden surface of the guitar neck shrinks as the guitar loses humidity; metal frets do not. Other signs that your guitar is losing moisture include the action lowering, causing buzzing when playing fretted or open strings, and the natural curve of the guitar back flattening out.

When a guitar is stored in dry conditions, the wood contracts, putting the soundboard, back, and sides at risk of cracking. In northern climates, low humidity and extreme cold occur in tandem. If at all possible, avoid bringing your guitar out in below freezing conditions. At a minimum, warm up the vehicle prior to loading an instrument. If your guitar is exposed to extreme cold, keep it in the case when returning indoors so the temperature can gradually readjust. Avoid extreme sudden changes in temperature, as that will cause your guitar to crack. If your guitar develops a crack, it can be repaired. Keep the surface clean, avoid touching it, as the oils on our hands will transfer to the wood, and take it to a qualified luthier for repair as soon as possible.

Humid Climate and Heat

The action rising and the guitar becoming more difficult to play are initial signs an instrument is suffering from too much humidity. The guitar may start to sound muffled as the extra humidity in the soundboard makes it less free to vibrate.

High humidity increases the moisture content of the wood, causing it to expand. The soundboard and back of the guitar may start to bulge and become uneven. The wood expands with increased humidity, but the joints that are glued together remain constant. In the worst-case scenario, pressure from expanding wood can cause cracks in the guitar, the neck to bend out of shape, and joints to become unglued. Cracks and changes in your guitar due to humidity can be repaired. Take your instrument to a qualified guitar maker for advice.

As with extreme cold, extreme heat will damage your guitar. I've seen more than one instrument with a melted finish as a result of being stored in a hot car on a summer day. Use caution. If it is too hot for a person or pet to stay in a closed car, it's too hot for your guitar.

Storage Solutions

Control humidity levels in your guitar case, and you'll improve the condition of your guitar. Hard-shell cases are most effective in maintaining consistent humidity levels. Purchase a portable *hygrometer*, an instrument that measures humidity, and install it in your case. Many small devices that attach to the inside of your case with Velcro are on the market. Leave the hygrometer in the case and guard against fluctuations in humidity levels.

If the level is low, introduce humidity to the case by using commercially available humidifiers, or make your own. Take a small plastic container, like a 35 mm film canister, poke holes in the plastic, cut a sponge to fit inside the container, and dampen the sponge. Ring out the sponge to ensure that water is not dripping. Depending on the canister size, suspend it over the soundhole by placing it between two adjacent strings, or use Velcro to attach it to the inside of your case. Find a spot where the canister will not come in direct contact with the wood of your guitar. Check the sponge periodically. When it dries out, re-moisten and ring out the sponge to avoid water dripping onto your guitar.

If the humidity level in your case is too high, place a humidity-observing product in your case. You can use silica gel packets or purchase one of the commercially available products specifically designed to lower the humidity of musical instruments.

Since you are controlling the humidity level in your case, always keep your instrument in the case with the top closed whenever you are not playing or practicing. When using your guitar, keep the empty guitar case closed so that the humidity level remains constant.

Cleaning

With consistent practice and playing, your guitar will need cleaning. Guitars finished with French-polished shellac, water-based lacquer, and synthetic varnishes can be cleaned with a slightly damp cloth and a small amount of dishwater soap. Clean a small area at a time and don't leave standing water anywhere on the guitar. Immediately wipe the guitar dry. **Caution:** this system does not work well on guitars with oil-based varnishes.

With use, your frets and fretboard may also get dirty. Use superfine, 0000-grade steel wool. It's available in most hardware stores. Remove or loosen the strings so that they are not on the fretboard. Rub the fretboard, wood, and frets with a little piece of the steel wool. This will clean the dirt and finger residue from the fingerboard and polish the frets. The superfine-grade steel wool won't leave any marks on the hard surface of the fretboard, but be careful so as not to rub on the varnish or the soundboard as you polish above the 12th fret.

Scratches

A scratch on the finish of your guitar does not adversely affect the sound, playability, or quality of your instrument. It does, however, ruin your mood. If the scratch is deep enough to extend through the guitar finish and damage the wood, take it to a skilled luthier for repair. If it's a cosmetic blemish, consider the scratch as proof that the guitar was played and loved.

LESSON #86: "COME AWAY" (DOWLAND)

John Dowland (1563–1636), the English Renaissance lutenist and composer, was arguably the most famous musician of his time. Dowland played a Renaissance lute with a tuning that is easily adapted to our modern-day guitar.

The Renaissance lute was strung with double courses, like a 12-string guitar. The highest string was always strung with a single course, called the *chanterelle*.

We don't know the exact pitch of the Renaissance lute, but it is clear that the intervals between the strings were the same as the modern-day guitar, with the third string tuned down a half step, to F♯. Occasionally, Dowland used a lute with added lower strings, or *diapasons*. "Come Away" was written for a seven-course lute, with the added string tuned a whole step below the sixth string.

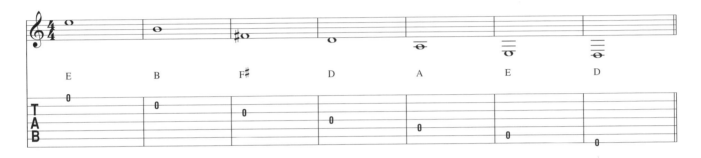

"Come Away" is Dowland's solo lute arrangement of his own choral work, "Come Again." Written in 1597, Dowland's *First Booke of Songes or Ayres* contains two versions of the song "Come Again," one written for lute and vocal soloist, and the other written for three-part choir: alto, tenor, and bass.

The anonymous lyrics deal with the subject of unrequited love:

Verse 1:

Come again! Sweet love doth now invite

Thy graces that refrain

To do me due delight

To see, to hear, to touch, to kiss, to die

With thee again in sweetest sympathy

Performance Notes

Tune the third string down a half step to F♯. Although the piece can be played in standard guitar tuning, the lowered third string facilitates fingering.

▶ **Measures 2–3:** Slide the third finger from C♯ to D for a smooth connection.

▶ **Measure 2, beat 4:** This is a characteristic cadential figure in Dowland's music. Although the notes are articulated as four 16ths, the second 16th note, D, rings over and connects to the C♯. The eighth note, G, is in the treble voice and resolves to the F♯ in measure 3. Dowland uses a similar figure in measure 12, beat 3.

▶ **Measure 5:** Play the F♯ with a hinge bar. Flatten out your first finger so it touches the first and second string. Lift the hinge bar at the beginning of beat 2, keeping your first finger on the C♯.

▶ **Measures 14–19:** an ornamented repeat of measures 8–13.

COME AWAY

John Dowland

Tuning:
(low to high) E-A-D-F#-B-E

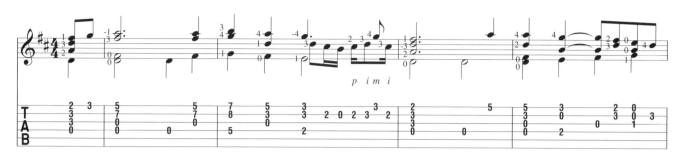

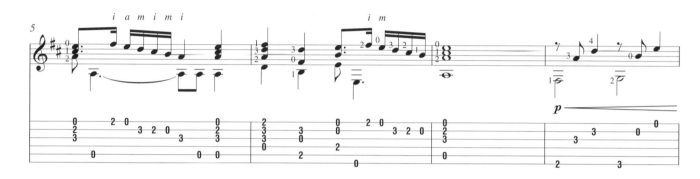

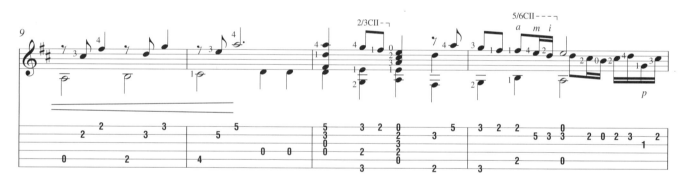

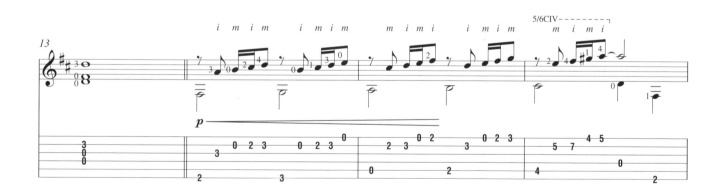

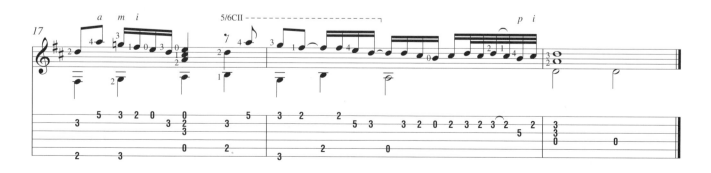

LESSON #87: "LÁGRIMA" (TÁRREGA)

The great Spanish guitarist and composer Francisco Tárrega (1852–1909) is one of the most influential figures of modern-day classical guitar. He worked closely with luthier Antonio de Torres (1817–1892) to develop and improve classical guitar construction, and his style of playing is the basis for our modern-day technique. Tárrega did not write a formal method, but his teaching is passed down through his students, two of whom, Emilio Pujol (1886–1980) and Pascual Roch (1860–1921), wrote important guitar method books.

Tárrega composed "Lágrima" in the style of a Romantic-era character piece. These short, personal, solo piano works were written to express non-musical ideas and feelings. *Rubato* literally translates to mean "stolen time." It is a relaxation of the strict pulse in order to express musical content and the personal meaning of a piece. Enjoy using rubato as you play "Lágrima." Stay aware of the beat, and after you "steal" time, return the piece to a steady pulse.

Lágrima means "tear." Tárrega expresses the image of a falling teardrop with the descending 4th, B–F♯, between the first two measures. Express the beauty of the descending 4th with a touch of rubato, then return to tempo.

▶ **Measures 1–5:** Emphasize the melody and keep accompaniment notes in the background. Use rest strokes to bring out the melody (notes with stems pointed up). Play the inner line and bass notes with free strokes.

▶ **Measure 6, beat 2:** Here is an example of cross-string fingering that works well. Play the half-note C♯ on the 11th fret, fourth string. Keep the C♯ ringing while you play the open E, F♯ on the third string, and A on the second string.

▶ **Measure 9:** The B-section moves to the key of E minor. Be sure to observe the accidentals.

▶ **Measure 10:** The open E on beat 1 is the melody note. Keep the E ringing while you play the moving 3rds.

▶ **Measure 12:** Like measure 10, the chord articulated on beat 1 continues ringing while the inner voice is played.

▶ **Measure 13:** This phrase begins with F♯, the last eighth note of measure 12. Similar to the beginning of the piece, use rest strokes to emphasize the melody.

LÁGRIMA

Francisco Tárrega

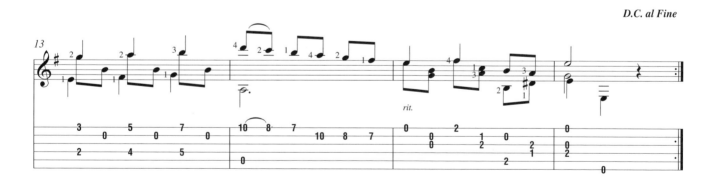

LESSON #88: LEFT-HAND POSITION

Let's face it—classical guitar music is challenging. Much of the repertoire contains complex lines, multiple voices, fast passages, and difficult chord shapes. To play effectively, we have to start with a relaxed, responsive, and effective left-hand position.

Arm Position

Try this exercise: hold your left-hand fingers in your right hand. Raise your left hand to eye level and completely relax your left arm. With your right hand holding up your left arm, notice the alignment of your wrist, fingers, and elbow. All are in a straight line and your shoulder is comfortably relaxed, neither reaching forward nor pulled back behind you.

The classical guitar sitting position, with the neck slanted upward and tuning pegs at eye level, promotes an optimal left-hand playing position.

As seen in the adjacent photo, when the neck of the guitar is raised, you can play from a relaxed position, with a straight left-hand wrist (not arched out in front of the guitar or collapsed back behind the fretboard) and a relaxed shoulder.

Finger Placement

Let's start by setting up your fingers for a perfectly relaxed position at the fifth fret.

Line your fingers up on the third string: first finger on the fifth fret, second finger on the sixth fret, third finger on the seventh fret, and fourth finger on the eighth fret.

Your second and third fingers sit almost perpendicular to the string, your first finger leans a little bit towards the headstock, and your fourth finger leans a little toward the bridge. Place your fingers as close to the upper fret as possible without touching the fret wire. Keep a natural curve to your fingers. If you end up touching the second string, raise the palm of your hand so that it is a little closer to the guitar. This will help curve your fingers.

Thumb Position

Make sure that your left-hand thumb rests lightly on the back of the guitar. It is a counter-weight or place holder and is used for balance, not to exert pressure or squeeze the neck.

Place your thumb on the back of the neck, between the first and second fingers. The specific shape of your hand will determine the exact location. Keep your thumb straight and rest the entire finger on the neck. Your thumb may point straight up to the ceiling, but is more likely to angle slightly toward the headstock.

Adjustments

The demands of even the simplest piece of classical guitar music will require you to adjust your general position.

Moving from a higher to lower string, as in a descending scale, takes more of the guitar neck into your hand. Slide your thumb higher on the neck (toward the ceiling) as your arm raises to access the lower string. As you play the ascending scale, slide your thumb towards the floor as your entire arm lowers.

When you have two or more fingers playing on the same fret, as in the open A chord, you'll need to adjust the angle of your hand. Move your elbow slightly away from your body. Your wrist will move and it will be easy to place three fingers in the second fret.

LESSON #89: MEMORIZATION

There is nothing more satisfying than performing a piece from memory with confidence and musicality. There is nothing worse than having a "memory slip" in a piece that you know and can play well. Memorization can be a mercurial talent; sometimes we seem to have it, sometimes we don't. In reality, memorization is a skill that we can study, work, and improve.

In order to perform confidently from memory, we need to build a fail-safe system, using more than one method or approach to memorizing a piece. Use all four of these memorization techniques to increase your skill and confidence when performing from memory.

Aural Memory

The first level of memorization is the ability to remember the tune or sound of the piece. What was it that drew you to the composition in the first place? Can you sing the primary melodic content of the piece and recall the interesting textures of each section? If the answer is "yes," then you're laying down the first layer of a secure memorization.

Motor/Muscle Memory

Every time you play a section of a piece, you are building motor, or muscle, memory. This memory works on a subconscious level and makes it possible for you to effortlessly perform the complex muscle movements needed to produce any note on the instrument. After learning a specific technique, chord shape, or scale pattern, muscle memory takes over, condensing all the information into a single impulse.

When you practice a passage or run through an entire piece, your muscle memory links one movement to the next, similar to the links of a chain-link fence. Your muscle memory does not evaluate what you are doing, but simply stores the movements. It creates a literal and strong record of how you have practiced. For best results, practice each section with the same fingering every time. If you choose to change your fingering later, you will need to carefully re-program your muscle memory.

Muscle memory works well until we become conscious of what we are doing. Have you had the experience of knowing a piece from memory, but when interrupted in the middle of a section, you can't find the next note or chord? This occurs because your muscle memory works on a subconscious level. Once links in your memory are interrupted, you became conscious of what you are doing and the muscle memory breaks down.

Luckily, you can use several conscious tools to trigger muscle memory and create a reliable system for memorizing music.

Analytical Memory

The better you know a piece of music, the easier it will be to memorize it.

FORM

Do you know the form of the piece? Are there sections or themes that repeat? When the music repeats, is it exactly the same, or slightly different? Create an internal roadmap of the piece so that you can identify where you are in the form and where you are going.

HARMONIC ANALYSIS/TONALITY IDENTIFICATION

Once you identify the form and how a piece is put together, delve in deeper to identify the sonority of the music. Are there any chord shapes that you can identify and remember? Are there chord shapes and progressions that reoccur? Is there a specific bass line that you can remember? The more details that you can identify, the stronger your analytical memory.

Visualization

Visualization is the ability to recreate the performance of the piece in your mind, without the reinforcement and feedback of playing it on the instrument. Start with a short section of the piece. Without the printed score or fingering the passage on the guitar, *play* the music in your mind. See your left-hand fingers accurately placed on the fingerboard, feel your specific right-hand fingering, and hear the music as you slowly recreate every aspect of the piece in your mind.

You are visualizing how your hands feel and look from the perspective of the performer. Avoid memorizing the way the music looks on the page.

This is a difficult task. Begin visualizing just a measure or two. After you successfully recreate the section in your head, reinforce the memory by playing it very slowly on the guitar. Then try adding a few more measures to your visualization.

Summary

To present a confident and secure memorized performance, you need to combine a strong aural, muscle, and analytical memory. You need the muscle memory to execute your technique. Aural memory contains the emotional content and meaning of your performance. Your analytical memory directs the performance and follows the roadmap of the music. Visualization confirms your knowledge of the piece and keeps you in control of your own music-making.

LESSON #90: "MRS. WINTER'S JUMP" (DOWLAND)

John Dowland (1563–1636), the English Renaissance lutenist and composer, was arguably the most famous musician of his time. Dowland played a Renaissance lute with a tuning that is easily adapted to our modern-day guitar. Dowland's instrument was tuned similarly to our modern-day guitar, with the third string dropped a half step, from G to F♯.

"Mrs. Winter's Jump" is a dance written in 6/8 meter, which is to be felt in two beats. Especially interesting are the ornaments that Dowland notated in the original manuscript: the "shake," found in measures 2, 3, 4, 6, 8, 12, and 16, and the "fall," notated in measure 10. These ornaments have been written out in the following score as grace notes. Play the first note of each ornament on the beat with the accompanying bass note (if applicable). Slur the following two notes, playing the ornament as quickly as possible. The following arrangement is adapted for standard-tuned guitar.

MRS. WINTER'S JUMP

John Dowland

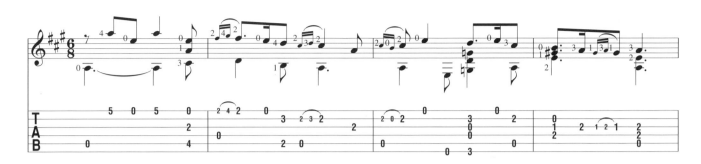

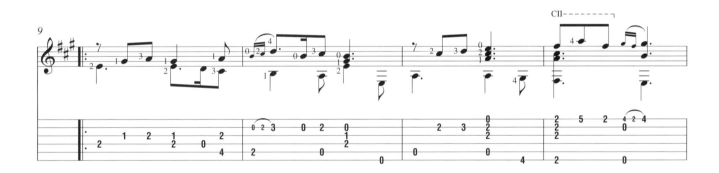

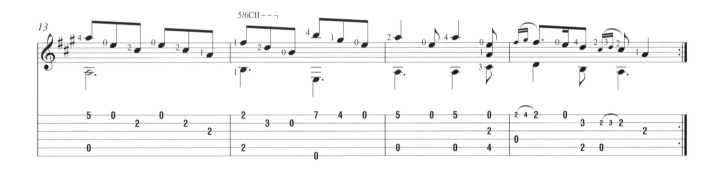

Spanish Renaissance composer Luis de Milán (1500–1561) played and composed for the vihuela. The *vihuela*, a precursor to the guitar, was popular in Spain and Italy during the 15th and 16th centuries. Like the lute, which was played in England and Europe, the vihuela is a six-course instrument. Each course, except for the first, is doubled. The tuning is similar to our modern-day classical guitar, with the third string tuned down a half step to F♯.

A slow courtly dance, "Pavana I" should be played at a moderate tempo. In measure 2, be sure to damp the E bass note so it does not ring into the A minor chord. Measure 35 is the most difficult passage of the piece. Isolate the scale passage for additional practice. Use the right-hand fingering as marked.

PAVANA I

Luis de Milán

LESSON #92: PRACTICING VS. PLAYING

As a teenager, I took piano lessons from an instructor who wanted to teach me the difference between practicing and playing. During one practice session, he stood outside my practice room door and anytime he heard me mindlessly playing through a piece of music instead of practicing, he barged in, arms flailing, and yelling. This may not have been the most evolved or popular teaching method, but I've never forgotten that lesson. Playing is not practicing.

Goal-Oriented Practice

Always practice with a goal in mind. When working on technique, your goal may be to learn a new scale pattern, improve speed and facility, or increase endurance. Create specific exercises to accomplish these goals, and always be aware of how and why you are practicing.

Repetition is an essential part of practicing, but practice wisely. Mindless repetition will result in acquiring bad habits. If you are working to increase speed, use a metronome. Start the exercise at a comfortable speed at which you can play the passage successfully several times in a row. Increase metronome speed by small increments and repeat the passage. Once you reach a speed at which you can no longer accurately and easily play the exercise, stop. Play short excerpts from the passage and, if possible, link smaller sections together at this faster speed. Even though you are practicing to increase speed, never play faster than you can control.

Your Brain on Music

Our brains are like computers. What we do in our practice sessions is programmed into the hard drive, right or wrong, and influences the outcome. Take care so as to only program accurate information. When learning a new piece, it's tempting to play through it many times in an attempt to get it into our fingers. Instead, take time to accurately learn the rhythms and pitches and to decide on right- and left-hand fingerings. If you program correct information from the start, you will never have to go through the arduous task of unlearning a mistake.

Problem-Area Practice

Every piece of music will have at least one difficult section. Instead of playing through an entire section or piece, streamline your practice by identifying the trouble spots and practicing them separately. I used to circle problem areas in the music with a red pencil. It was a good way to identify what I needed to practice, but once the problem spot was mastered, the red circle remained, increasing my tension as I approached what used to be a difficult section. Instead of marking the score, use sticky notes to identify problem spots. The cheerful colors will remind you to practice the hard spots first. Once the problem spot is mastered, move the sticky to the next problem area, because a new hard spot will always appear.

Practice Performing

Before playing in public, practice performing. Playing to a live audience or making a recording is very different from practicing. When you perform, turn off your judgments and suspend all evaluations. Your concentration will improve if you set one specific goal for a performance such as bringing out dynamic changes, settling into a consistent and steady tempo, or connecting all melodic lines. Focus on making music and the technical elements you have diligently practiced will take care of themselves.

Record a piece or your entire program. Listening to the recording will help you identify problem spots and evaluate the effectiveness of your interpretation, articulations, dynamics, and tone-color changes. Make notes of your observations, as this will serve as a to-do list for your next practice session. Identify any lapses in concentration or memory slips. If this happens at a specific spot in the music, examine the section and identify musical elements to focus on.

Once satisfied with your recordings, recruit a small but friendly audience to play for. Remember to suspend all judgment as you perform. Your job is to focus on your performance, not to judge your playing. The audience will give you feedback. If a member of your audience is a musician, provide them with a score and ask them to write in any comments they may have.

Playing is not practicing, but both can be enjoyed. Celebrate the accomplishments that you make in your practice sessions and know that effective practice is the only path to a successful performance.

LESSON #93: PRODUCTIVE PRACTICE

As a classical guitarist we spend the majority of our rehearsal time in solo practice—we rarely rehearse with a professional conductor who models excellent practice procedures, nor do we discuss the banal details of our practice procedures with other musicians. Let's pull back the curtain and discuss how we can make the most of our limited practice time.

Consistent Practice Is Key

I once had a teacher who said, "Practicing today prepares you to practice better tomorrow." Daily practice improves technique and is the key to mastering new repertoire. It's better to practice an hour or two several days in a row than six hours in one day. When we practice, we train our mind and muscles to perform. As with sports, we need to reinforce this training on a daily basis.

My practice schedule consists of 60–90 minute blocks. When possible, I practice first thing in the morning so my mind is fresh and not distracted by life and work. When I start the day playing my guitar, I am likely to sit down in the evening or late afternoon and continue the work I started. Many of my students and colleagues prefer to practice in the evening. At the end of a day, they are able to turn their full attention to the instrument. It is not important what time of day you practice, but it is important to make time for your music. Make it a priority in your schedule and purposefully reserve time for your craft. I have never heard a musician say, "I have nothing else to do, so I think I'll practice today."

Create a Good Practice Space

Your practice space does not have to be elaborate, but make sure that you have the bare-bone essentials.

Use a good chair when you practice—a hard chair or bench that allows you to sit in a comfortable classical position. Like *Goldilocks and the Three Bears*, the chair should not be too tall or too short. The posture and sitting position that you use in practice should be as close as possible to the position you use in performance. Prior to a concert, practice in the clothes and shoes that you will wear at the performance. A jacket may restrict your movements, and shoes with heels may change your sitting position.

Make sure that you have ample light to see your music and an appropriate method of supporting the score. Laying the music flat on a table or desk causes you to strain your neck to see the notes. Use a music stand or similar device to prop up your music. Many musicians today read their printed music from tablets—a great idea as long as the music is easy to read.

You'll need a pencil to mark in fingerings, a notepad to write down ideas for your next practice session, as well as a metronome and a recording/playback device.

Technique Practice

Technical facility on the guitar is a long-term goal. As long as you are a guitarist, you will spend time working on scales, slurs, and right-hand arpeggios. Use a metronome and record the speed of your scales and arpeggio patterns in a notebook. Over time, you'll be encouraged by your progress. Be honest in your recordkeeping. You'll find that, when you have less time to focus on technique, your speed and accuracy diminish.

Build Your Repertoire

Pick repertoire appropriate for your skill. If it takes you longer than four weeks to learn a piece, you are working on music that is too hard. Successfully learning easier pieces helps prepare you to play more difficult repertoire. Choose a variety of music from different time periods to broaden your musical vocabulary and interpretive skills. Follow these general guidelines (not in any strict order) to successfully learn a new piece of music:

- Listen to several recordings of the piece. If you are learning a transcription originally written for another instrument, listen to recordings of the original instrumentation, as well as guitar recordings.

- Read through the piece in its entirety or in smaller sections. Make preliminary decisions on right- and left-hand fingerings, then pencil them in.

- Identify the form and structure of the piece. Learn about the composer, musical period, and historical performance practice.

- Play through the piece with a metronome.

- Identify problem spots. Isolate difficult sections and work on them separately.

- Memorize the composition.

Like a conductor preparing to rehearse a symphony orchestra, approach every practice session with a plan. Write down problem spots that require attention, then practice those first. When you are about done for the day, record the piece or section you've been working on and identify goals for the next practice session.

You're Only as Good as Your Information

Instructional books and internet videos for playing the classical guitar are readily available, but nothing is as valuable as a good teacher. Don't reinvent the wheel by trying to learn on your own; instead, seek out good information from a qualified teacher. An experienced mentor will provide you with personalized feedback, prevent you from acquiring bad habits, and guide you to a higher level of playing.

LESSON #94: REST STROKE VS. FREE STROKE

Classical guitarists use two basic strokes to produce sound with the right hand: rest stroke and free stroke. *Rest stroke*, also called the "supported stroke," or *apoyando* in Spanish, is effective at emphasizing a particular note or voice, bringing out a melodic line, and for playing scale passages. *Free stroke*, also called the "escape stroke," or *tirando* in Spanish, is used to play chords, arpeggios, accompaniments, and inner lines of a texture.

Rest Stroke

MECHANICS

1. Place you finger on the string

2. Push the string inward, towards your belly

3. Play/release the string

4. Follow through and rest the finger on the next, lower string

HAND POSITION

▶ When playing rest stroke with fingers, your wrist is lower (i.e., closer to the soundboard) than when playing free stroke. Your large knuckles (metacarpophalangeal joints) hover over the string, two or three strings lower than the one you are playing.

SOUND

▶ Aiming your finger towards and resting on the next, lower string creates a deep stroke, which produces a warm and resonant sound.

Free Stroke

MECHANICS

1. Place your finger on the string

2. Push the string inward, towards your belly

3. Play/release the string

4. Follow through, with the finger coming towards the palm of your hand, escaping the next, lower string

HAND POSITION

▶ When playing free stroke with the fingers, your large knuckles (metacarpophalangeal joints) hover over the string you are playing.

SOUND

▶ When playing free stroke, you avoid damping the next, lower string. Notes on adjacent strings can ring out.

Rest Stroke with *i*, *m*, and *a* Fingers	Free Stroke with *i*, *m*, and *a* Fingers
Position your hand so that your knuckles hover over the string, two or three strings lower than the one you are playing.	Position your hand so that your knuckles are above the string you are playing.
Push the string inward, toward your belly.	Push the string inward, toward your belly.
Follow through, with your finger touching/resting on the next, lower string.	Follow through and avoid touching the next, lower string.
Used for single-line melodies, to bring out a line, accented notes, and scale passages.	Used for chords, arpeggios, any two notes on adjacent strings, inner lines, and accompaniments.

Matteo Carcassi's (1792–1853) *Study, Op. 60, No. 16*: use rest stroke to bring out the melody and free stroke to play the accompaniment.

EXAMPLE 1

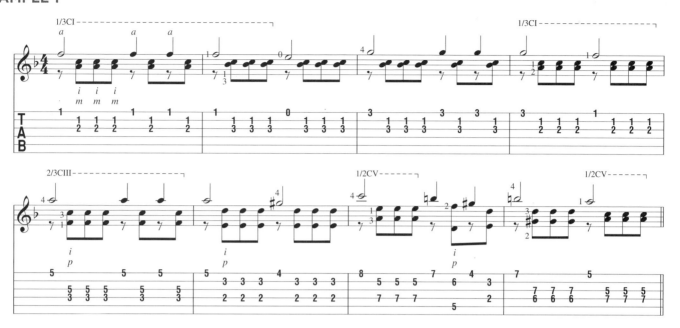

Mauro Giuliani's (1781–1829) *Etude, No. 5, Op. 48*: an example of broken chords/arpeggios. Use free stroke exclusively.

EXAMPLE 2

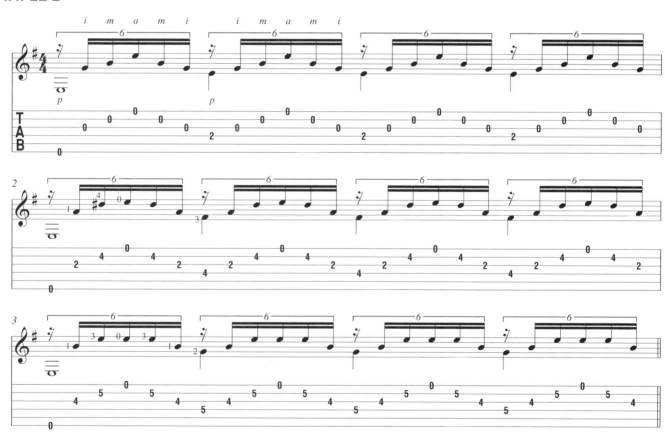

Luis de Milán's (1500–1561) *Pavana*: an example of blocked chords. Use free stroke exclusively.

EXAMPLE 3

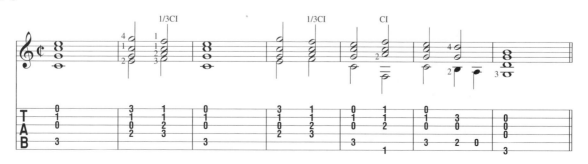

"DANCE DE LAS HACHAS" (SANZ)

Gaspar Sanz (1640–1710), the great Spanish Baroque guitarist, played a five-course guitar. This instrument was smaller than our modern-day classical guitar and popular in Spain, France, and Italy during the Baroque era.

Baroque guitarists employed a variety of different tunings, and without a low sixth string, the instrument had a bright and cheerful sound. Sanz used the most popular Baroque guitar tuning for all of his compositions: the first course is a single string, the second course is two strings in unison, the third course is two strings in unison, the fourth course is two strings an octave apart, and the fifth course is two strings in unison but tuned a fifth above the fourth string.

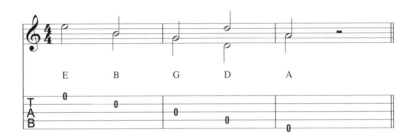

Dance de las Hachas, or "Dance of the Axes," is the second piece in Sanz's second book, *Libro segundo, de cifras sobre la guitarra española*. As you can see from the photo of Sanz's original manuscript, the music is written in tablature. Different than modern-day guitar tablature, the highest-sounding string is written at the bottom of the tab.

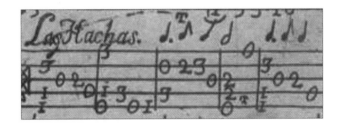

Joaquín Rodrigo quotes this piece in his famous *Fantasia para Gentilhombre* for guitar and orchestra. *Danza de las Hachas* is the third movement of Rodrigo's work.

Below is an arrangement of the piece based on the original Baroque guitar tablature. Baroque guitarists used improvised rhythmic strumming patterns. Experiment performing the chords with different strumming techniques.

DANCE DE LAS HACHAS

Gaspar Sanz

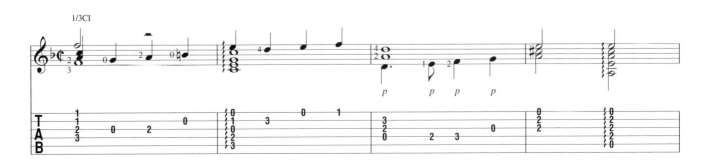

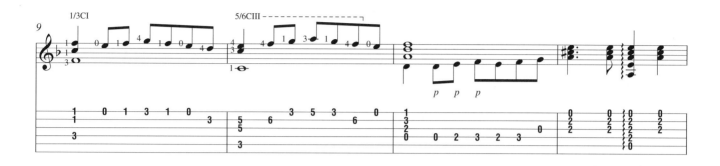

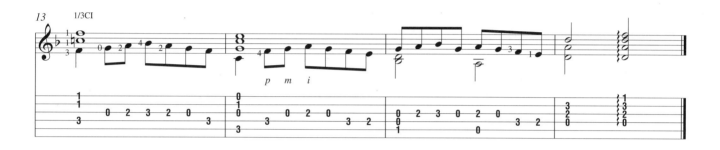

LESSON #96: ANDRÉS SEGOVIA

Photo: Jac. de Nijs / Anefo

Andrés Segovia (1893–1987) is arguably the most influential guitarist of our time. Born in Linares, Spain, Segovia claimed to be self-taught. He was passionate about the guitar and worked tirelessly to raise the status of his chosen instrument.

Segovia's significant accomplishments can be divided into three distinct categories:

1. Expand the classical guitar repertoire.

2. Establish the guitar as a major concert instrument.

3. Ensure the education of future classical guitar performers.

Repertoire

Segovia's early concert programs consisted of music originally written for guitar by Napoléon Coste, Fernando Sor, and Francisco Tárrega. Also featured were Tárrega's and Miguel Llobet's transcriptions of works by Bach, Beethoven, Granados, Schumann, and others. As Segovia's concert career progressed, he worked to expand the classical guitar repertoire, performing and publishing his own transcriptions, including works by Fescobaldi, Couperin, Handel, and Bach. Segovia's most influential transcription was his version of J.S. Bach's "Chaconne," from *Violin Partita No. 2, BWV 1004*.

Segovia created long-lasting friendships with his contemporary composers, many of whom he convinced to compose pieces for the guitar. Joaquín Rodrigo (1901–1999), Joaquín Turina (1882–1949), Federico Moreno Torroba (1891–1982), Alexandre Tansman (1897–1986), Mario Castelnuovo-Tedesco (1895–1968), and Heitor Villa-Lobos (1887–1959) all wrote pieces for Andrés Segovia.

Mexican composer Manuel Ponce (1882–1948) had a very close relationship with Segovia, as illustrated in a collection of letters written by the guitarist to the composer and published in *The Segovia-Ponce Letters,* edited by Miguel Alcázar and translated by Peter Segal. An active composer for piano, voice, and orchestra, it wasn't until he met Andrés Segovia in 1923 that Ponce began to compose for the guitar. Segovia encouraged Ponce to compose specific genres of pieces, made suggestions throughout the development of Ponce's compositions, and edited the works for performance and publication. The Segovia/Ponce collaboration resulted in Ponce composing over 30 works for solo guitar, including three sonatas and the famous *Concierto del Sur* for guitar and orchestra, which Segovia premiered on October 9, 1941.

Concerts

Segovia gave his first public performance in 1909, when he was only 16. He continued to gain success and notoriety and made his debut performance in New York in 1928. This concert led to further tours throughout the U.S., Europe, and Asia.

Segovia helped to improve the construction of classical guitars. He worked closely with German luthier Herman Hauser Sr. and Spanish luthier Jose Ramirez. After World War II, Segovia changed from using gut strings to improved nylon strings on his guitar. The nylon provided improved intonation and increased volume.

With a concert-level instrument and expanded classical repertoire, Segovia raised the level of the classical guitar to that of a serious concert instrument and introduced the guitar to new audiences and venues.

Education

Even with his busy concert schedule, Segovia made teaching a priority. He held master classes at the *Música en Compostela* in the northern Spanish city of Santiago de Compostela and in Siena, Italy, at *Accademia Musicale Chigiana*. Segovia's influence and instruction reaches beyond the students who studied directly with him. Those students went on to teach at major universities and conservatories throughout the U.S. and Europe, spreading Segovia's information and influence to younger generations of guitarists.

Legacy

Segovia had a long and productive career. He recorded his last LP, *Reveries* (RCA), when he was 84 and had concerts scheduled up until his death at the age of 94.

With such a long career, it would be surprising for Segovia to have escaped all criticism. Some say he was a dogmatic teacher, ignored important concert guitarists in South America, including Agustín Barrios Mangoré, and, although many composers wrote music for him, Segovia only performed those selections that met his musical taste and sensibilities.

Regardless of the criticism, Segovia is a pivotal figure in the world of classical guitar. No current player can escape his great influence.

"TOY FOR TWO LUTES" (ROBINSON)

English lutenist Thomas Robinson (1560–1610) was a prominent performer and pedagogue. "Toy for Two Lutes" was originally written for a seven-course lute. Robinson's lute was tuned similar to our modern-day guitar, with the third string lowered to an F♯ and the seventh string tuned a whole step below the sixth string. "Toy" is a common Renaissance title for a light piece usually written for lute or *virginal* (keyboard instrument).

The original manuscript is 32 measures long. Each four-bar phrase is written out with the voices switching parts. Perform this toy with a duet partner (and in standard tuning). Play guitar 1 for measures 1–4. Take the repeat and play guitar 2 while your partner performs guitar 1. At measure 5, return to guitar 1, switching to guitar 2 at the repeat.

 GUITAR 1 ONLY

 GUITAR DUET

TOY FOR TWO LUTES

Thomas Robinson

VALTZ, SONATA NO. 20 (PAGANINI)

The Italian violin virtuoso Niccolò Paganini (1782–1840) was also a highly accomplished guitarist. He mainly played guitar privately, turning to the six-string instrument as a diversion from the violin and to work out ideas for other compositions. Paganini only occasionally performed guitar concerts in private homes, perhaps not wishing to advertise his prowess on the guitar and diluting his renown as a violinist.

Paganini's 100-plus compositions for guitar include 37 multi-movement sonatas, 43 *Ghiribizzi*, or "whims" (written for a young female guitar student who lived in Naples), as well as other solo guitar compositions and chamber music for guitar and string instruments.

Sonata 20 is a two-movement work: Minuetto and Valtz. The Valtz begins in C major, moves to A minor at measure 19, then returns to C major with the *Da Capo*.

Measure 2: Although not the most comfortable fingering, use fingers 2 and 3 on beat 1 so that the B can ring throughout the measure.

VALTZ, SONATA NO. 20

Niccolò Paganini

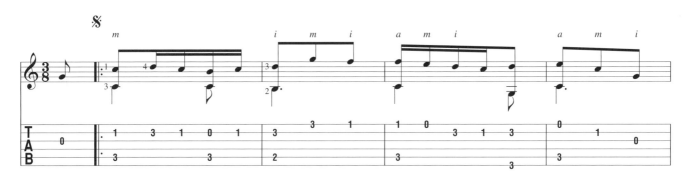

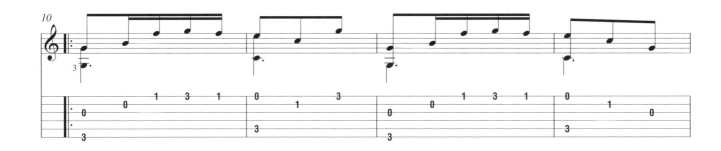

LESSON #99: VALTZ, SONATA NO. 27 (PAGANINI)

The Italian violin virtuoso Niccolò Paganini (1782–1840) was also a highly accomplished guitarist. He mainly played guitar privately, turning to the six-string instrument as a diversion from the violin and to work out ideas for other compositions. Paganini only occasionally performed guitar concerts in private homes, perhaps not wishing to advertise his prowess on the guitar and diluting his renown as a violinist. He composed over 100 pieces for solo guitar. Not as difficult as his virtuosic violin compositions, Paganini's guitar music is charming and approachable.

Sonata 27 is a two-movement work: *Minuetto per la Signora Marina and Valtz.*

The Valtz is an optimistic piece written in 3/8. Feel each measure as a single pulse to bring out the feeling of the dance.

▶ **Measure 13:** Play the G♯ grace note on the beat with the D bass note.

▶ Paganini did not include dynamic markings in his guitar music. On the repeat, change the dynamics and/or tone color to create interest and variety.

VALTZ, SONATA NO. 27

Niccolò Paganini

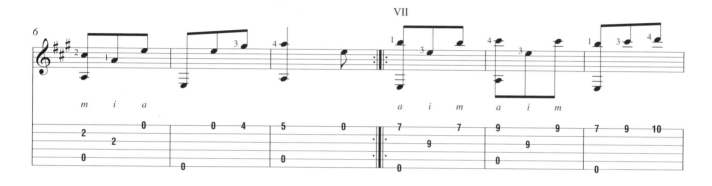

LESSON #100: "ZARABANDE" (SANZ)

Gaspar Sanz (1640–1710), the great Spanish Baroque guitarist, was a master of the five-course guitar. This instrument was smaller than our modern-day classical guitar and popular in Spain, France, and Italy during the Baroque era.

Baroque guitarists employed a variety of different tunings, and without a low sixth string, the instrument had a bright and cheerful sound. In his compositions, Sanz used the following guitar tuning: the first course is a single string, the second course is two strings in unison, the third course is two strings in unison, the fourth course is two strings an octave apart, and the fifth course is two strings in unison but tuned a fifth above the fourth string.

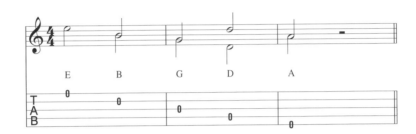

"Zarabande" is the seventh piece in Sanz's second book, *Libro segundo, de cifras sobre la guitarra española*. The original music is written in tablature. Different than modern-day guitar tablature, Sanz writes the highest-sounding string at the bottom of the tab.

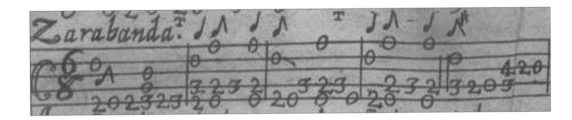

In the above photo of Sanz's original manuscript, you can clearly see the rhythmic notation written above the tab. The articulations continue at the same speed until a new rhythmic symbol appears. In measure 3, for instance, all notes are articulated as eighth notes.

"Zarabande" is written in 6/8, but on closer inspection, the measures alternate between 6/8 and 3/4. This type of rhythmic alternation is called *hemiola*. Practice clapping the rhythm, emphasizing the accented notes.

HEMIOLA

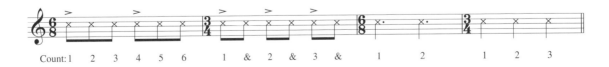

- **Measure 4:** Sanz marks the notation for a trill. Play the main F♯ note on the beat, slur up to G as quickly as possible, and then move back down to F♯.

- **Measure 7:** Similar to measure 4.

- **Measure 9:** The fingering may seem odd, but playing B on the open second string avoids an awkward shift.

ZARABANDE

Gaspar Sanz

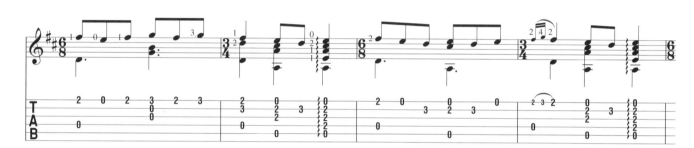

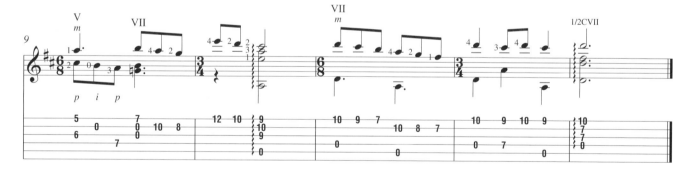

CLASSICAL GUITAR
PUBLICATIONS FROM HAL LEONARD

THE BEATLES FOR CLASSICAL GUITAR

Includes 20 solos from big Beatles hits arranged for classical guitar, complete with left-hand and right-hand fingering. Songs include: All My Loving • And I Love Her • Can't Buy Me Love • Fool on the Hill • From a Window • Hey Jude • If I Fell • Let It Be • Michelle • Norwegian Wood • Obla Di • Ticket to Ride • Yesterday • and more. Features arrangements and an introduction by Joe Washington, as well as his helpful hints on classical technique and detailed notes on how to play each song. The book also covers parts and specifications of the classical guitar, tuning, and Joe's "Strata System" – an easy-reading system applied to chord diagrams.

00699237 Classical Guitar $19.99

CZERNY FOR GUITAR
INCLUDES TAB

12 SCALE STUDIES FOR CLASSICAL GUITAR

by David Patterson

Adapted from Carl Czerny's *School of Velocity, Op. 299* for piano, this lesson book explores 12 keys with 12 different approaches or "treatments." You will explore a variety of articulations, ranges and technical perspectives as you learn each key. These arrangements will not only improve your ability to play scales fluently, but will also develop your ears, knowledge of the fingerboard, reading abilities, strength and endurance. In standard notation and tablature.

00701248 ....$9.99

MATTEO CARCASSI – 25 MELODIC AND PROGRESSIVE STUDIES, OP. 60

arr. Paul Henry

One of Carcassi's (1792-1853) most famous collections of classical guitar music – indispensable for the modern guitarist's musical and technical development. Performed by Paul Henry. 49-minute audio accompaniment.

00696506 Book/CD Pack.....................$17.95

CLASSICAL & FINGERSTYLE GUITAR TECHNIQUES
INCLUDES TAB

by David Oakes • Musicians Institute

This Master Class with MI instructor David Oakes is aimed at any electric or acoustic guitarist who wants a quick, thorough grounding in the essentials of classical and fingerstyle technique. Topics covered include: arpeggios and scales, free stroke and rest stroke, P-i scale technique, three-to-a-string patterns, natural and artificial harmonics, tremolo and rasgueado, and more. The book includes 12 intensive lessons for right and left hand in standard notation & tab, and the CD features 92 solo acoustic tracks.

00695171 Book/CD Pack......................$17.99

CLASSICAL GUITAR CHRISTMAS COLLECTION
INCLUDES TAB

Includes classical guitar arrangements in standard notation and tablature for more than two dozen beloved carols: Angels We Have Heard on High • Auld Lang Syne • Ave Maria • Away in a Manger • Canon in D • The First Noel • God Rest Ye Merry, Gentlemen • Hark! the Herald Angels Sing • I Saw Three Ships • Jesu, Joy of Man's Desiring • Joy to the World • O Christmas Tree • O Holy Night • Silent Night • What Child Is This? • and more.

00699493 Guitar Solo $10.99

CLASSICAL GUITAR WEDDING
INCLUDES TAB

Perfect for players hired to perform for someone's big day, this songbook features 16 classsical wedding favorites arranged for solo guitar in standard notation and tablature. Includes: Air on the G String • Ave Maria • Bridal Chorus • Canon in D • Jesu, Joy of Man's Desiring • Minuet • Sheep May Safely Graze • Wedding March • and more.

00699563 Solo Guitar with Tab...............$12.99

CLASSICAL MASTERPIECES FOR GUITAR
INCLUDES TAB

27 works by Bach, Beethoven, Handel, Mendelssohn, Mozart and more transcribed with standard notation and tablature. Now anyone can enjoy classical material regardless of their guitar background. Also features stay-open binding.

00699312 ....$12.95

MASTERWORKS FOR GUITAR
INCLUDES TAB

Over 60 Favorites from Four Centuries
World's Great Classical Music

Dozens of classical masterpieces: Allemande • Bourree • Canon in D • Jesu, Joy of Man's Desiring • Lagrima • Malaguena • Mazurka • Piano Sonata No. 14 in C# Minor (Moonlight) Op. 27 No. 2 First Movement Theme • Ode to Joy • Prelude No. I (Well-Tempered Clavier).

00699503 ....$16.95

A MODERN APPROACH TO CLASSICAL GUITAR

by Charles Duncan

This multi-volume method was developed to allow students to study the art of classical guitar within a new, more contemporary framework. For private, class or self-instruction. Book One incorporates chord frames and symbols, as well as a recording to assist in tuning and to provide accompaniments for at-home practice. Book One also introduces beginning fingerboard technique and music theory. Book Two and Three build upon the techniques learned in Book One.

00695114 Book 1 – Book Only $6.99
00695113 Book 1 – Book/Online Audio...............$10.99
00695116 Book 2 – Book Only $6.99
00695115 Book 2 – Book/Online Audio...............$10.99
00699202 Book 3 – Book Only $9.99
00695117 Book 3 – Book/CD Pack.....................$10.95
00695119 Composite Book/CD Pack $29.99

ANDRES SEGOVIA – 20 STUDIES FOR GUITAR

Sor/Segovia

20 studies for the classical guitar written by Beethoven's contemporary, Fernando Sor, revised, edited and fingered by the great classical guitarist Andres Segovia. These essential repertoire pieces continue to be used by teachers and students to build solid classical technique. Features a 50-minute demonstration CD.

_____ 00695012 Book/CD Pack $19.99
_____ 00006363 Book Only $7.99

THE FRANCISCO COLLECTION TÁRREGA
INCLUDES TAB

edited and performed by Paul Henry

Considered the father of modern classical guitar, Francisco Tárrega revolutionized guitar technique and composed a wealth of music that will be a cornerstone of classical guitar repertoire for centuries to come. This unique book/CD pack features 14 of his most outstanding pieces in standard notation and tab, edited and performed on CD by virtuoso Paul Henry. Includes: Adelita • Capricho Árabe • Estudio Brillante • Grand Jota • Lágrima • Malagueña • María • Recuerdos de la Alhambra • Tango • and more, plus bios of Tárrega and Henry.

_____ 00698993 Book/CD Pack $19.99

HAL•LEONARD®
CORPORATION

7777 W. BLUEMOUND RD. P.O. BOX 13819 MILWAUKEE, WI 53213

Visit Hal Leonard Online at **www.halleonard.com**

0616

Get Better at Guitar

...with these Great Guitar Instruction Books from Hal Leonard!

101 GUITAR TIPS
INCLUDES TAB

STUFF ALL THE PROS KNOW AND USE
by Adam St. James

This book contains invaluable guidance on everything from scales and music theory to truss rod adjustments, proper recording studio set-ups, and much more. The book also features snippets of advice from some of the most celebrated guitarists and producers in the music business, including B.B. King, Steve Vai, Joe Satriani, Warren Haynes, Laurence Juber, Pete Anderson, Tom Dowd and others, culled from the author's hundreds of interviews.

00695737 Book/Online Audio $16.99

AMAZING PHRASING
INCLUDES TAB

50 WAYS TO IMPROVE YOUR IMPROVISATIONAL SKILLS
by Tom Kolb

This book/CD pack explores all the main components necessary for crafting well-balanced rhythmic and melodic phrases. It also explains how these phrases are put together to form cohesive solos. Many styles are covered – rock, blues, jazz, fusion, country, Latin, funk and more – and all of the concepts are backed up with musical examples. The companion CD contains 89 demos for listening, and most tracks feature full-band backing.

00695583 Book/CD Pack..$19.95

BLUES YOU CAN USE – 2ND EDITION

by John Ganapes

This comprehensive source for learning blues guitar is designed to develop both your lead and rhythm playing. Includes: 21 complete solos • blues chords, progressions and riffs • turnarounds • movable scales and soloing techniques • string bending • utilizing the entire fingerboard • and more. This second edition now includes audio and video access online!

00142420 Book/Online Media................................$19.99

FRETBOARD MASTERY
INCLUDES TAB

by Troy Stetina

Untangle the mysterious regions of the guitar fretboard and unlock your potential. *Fretboard Mastery* familiarizes you with all the shapes you need to know by applying them in real musical examples, thereby reinforcing and reaffirming your newfound knowledge. The result is a much higher level of comprehension and retention.

00695331 Book/Online Audio $19.99

FRETBOARD ROADMAPS – 2ND EDITION

ESSENTIAL GUITAR PATTERNS THAT ALL THE PROS KNOW AND USE
by Fred Sokolow

The updated edition of this bestseller features more songs, updated lessons, and a full audio CD! Learn to play lead and rhythm anywhere on the fretboard, in any key; play a variety of lead guitar styles; play chords and progressions anywhere on the fretboard; expand your chord vocabulary; and learn to think musically – the way the pros do.

00695941 Book/CD Pack..$14.95

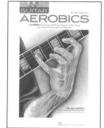

GUITAR AEROBICS
INCLUDES TAB

A 52-WEEK, ONE-LICK-PER-DAY WORKOUT PROGRAM FOR DEVELOPING, IMPROVING & MAINTAINING GUITAR TECHNIQUE
by Troy Nelson

From the former editor of *Guitar One* magazine, here is a daily dose of vitamins to keep your chops fine tuned! Musical styles include rock, blues, jazz, metal, country, and funk. Techniques taught include alternate picking, arpeggios, sweep picking, string skipping, legato, string bending, and rhythm guitar. These exercises will increase speed, and improve dexterity and pick- and fret-hand accuracy. The accompanying audio includes all 365 workout licks plus play-along grooves in every style at eight different metronome settings.

00695946 Book/Online Audio $19.99

GUITAR CLUES
INCLUDES TAB

OPERATION PENTATONIC
by Greg Koch

Join renowned guitar master Greg Koch as he clues you in to a wide variety of fun and valuable pentatonic scale applications. Whether you're new to improvising or have been doing it for a while, this book/CD pack will provide loads of delicious licks and tricks that you can use right away, from volume swells and chicken pickin' to intervallic and chordal ideas. The CD includes 65 demo and play-along tracks.

00695827 Book/CD Pack..$19.95

INTRODUCTION TO GUITAR TONE & EFFECTS

by David M. Brewster

This book/CD pack teaches the basics of guitar tones and effects, with audio examples on CD. Readers will learn about: overdrive, distortion and fuzz • using equalizers • modulation effects • reverb and delay • multi-effect processors • and more.

00695766 Book/CD Pack..$14.99

PICTURE CHORD ENCYCLOPEDIA

This comprehensive guitar chord resource for all playing styles and levels features five voicings of 44 chord qualities for all twelve keys – 2,640 chords in all! For each, there is a clearly illustrated chord frame, as well as *an actual photo* of the chord being played! Includes info on basic fingering principles, open chords and barre chords, partial chords and broken-set forms, and more.

00695224..$19.95

SCALE CHORD RELATIONSHIPS
INCLUDES TAB

by Michael Mueller & Jeff Schroedl

This book teaches players how to determine which scales to play with which chords, so guitarists will never have to fear chord changes again! This book/audio pack explains how to: recognize keys • analyze chord progressions • use the modes • play over nondiatonic harmony • use harmonic and melodic minor scales • use symmetrical scales such as chromatic, whole-tone and diminished scales • incorporate exotic scales such as Hungarian major and Gypsy minor • and much more!

00695563 Book/Online Audio $14.99

SPEED MECHANICS FOR LEAD GUITAR
INCLUDES TAB

Take your playing to the stratosphere with the most advanced lead book by this proven heavy metal author. *Speed Mechanics* is the ultimate technique book for developing the kind of speed and precision in today's explosive playing styles. Learn the fastest ways to achieve speed and control, secrets to make your practice time really count, and how to open your ears and make your musical ideas more solid and tangible. Packed with over 200 vicious exercises including Troy's scorching version of "Flight of the Bumblebee." Music and examples demonstrated on CD. 89-minute audio.

00699323 Book/CD Pack..$19.95

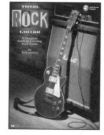

TOTAL ROCK GUITAR
INCLUDES TAB

A COMPLETE GUIDE TO LEARNING ROCK GUITAR
by Troy Stetina

This unique and comprehensive source for learning rock guitar is designed to develop both lead and rhythm playing. It covers: getting a tone that rocks • open chords, power chords and barre chords • riffs, scales and licks • string bending, strumming, palm muting, harmonics and alternate picking • all rock styles • and much more. The examples are in standard notation with chord grids and tab, and the audio includes full-band backing for all 22 songs.

00695246 Book/Online Audio $19.99

GUITAR PLAY-ALONG

AUDIO ACCESS INCLUDED

INCLUDES TAB

This series will help you play your favorite songs quickly and easily. Just follow the tab and listen to the CD or online audio to hear how the guitar should sound, and then play along using the separate backing tracks. Playback tools are provided for slowing down the tempo without changing pitch and looping challenging parts. The melody and lyrics are included in the book so that you can sing or simply follow along.

1. ROCK 00699570 .... $16.99	**21. YULETIDE** 00699602 .... $14.95	**40. INCUBUS** 00699668 .... $17.95	**61. SLIPKNOT** 00699775 .... $16.99
2. ACOUSTIC 00699569 .... $16.95	**22. CHRISTMAS** 00699600 .... $15.95	**41. ERIC CLAPTON** 00699669 .... $16.95	**62. CHRISTMAS CAROLS** 00699798 .... $12.95
3. HARD ROCK 00699573 .... $16.95	**23. SURF** 00699635 .... $14.95	**42. 2000s ROCK** 00699670 .... $16.99	**63. CREEDENCE CLEARWATER REVIVAL** 00699802 .... $16.99
4. POP/ROCK 00699571 .... $16.99	**24. ERIC CLAPTON** 00699649 .... $17.99	**43. LYNYRD SKYNYRD** 00699681 .... $17.95	**64. OZZY OSBOURNE** 00699803 .... $16.99
5. MODERN ROCK 00699574 .... $16.99	**25. LENNON & McCARTNEY** 00699642 .... $16.99	**44. JAZZ** 00699689 .... $14.99	**66. THE ROLLING STONES** 00699807 .... $16.95
6. '90s ROCK 00699572 .... $16.99	**26. ELVIS PRESLEY** 00699643 .... $14.95	**45. TV THEMES** 00699718 .... $14.95	**67. BLACK SABBATH** 00699808 .... $16.99
7. BLUES 00699575 .... $16.95	**27. DAVID LEE ROTH** 00699645 .... $16.95	**46. MAINSTREAM ROCK** 00699722 .... $16.95	**68. PINK FLOYD – DARK SIDE OF THE MOON** 00699809 .... $16.99
8. ROCK 00699585 .... $14.99	**28. GREG KOCH** 00699646 .... $14.95	**47. HENDRIX SMASH HITS** 00699723 .... $19.95	**69. ACOUSTIC FAVORITES** 00699810 .... $14.95
10. ACOUSTIC 00699586 .... $16.95	**29. BOB SEGER** 00699647 .... $15.99	**48. AEROSMITH CLASSICS** 00699724 .... $17.99	**70. OZZY OSBOURNE** 00699805 .... $16.99
11. EARLY ROCK 0699579 .... $14.95	**30. KISS** 00699644 .... $16.99	**49. STEVIE RAY VAUGHAN** 00699725 .... $17.99	**71. CHRISTIAN ROCK** 00699824 .... $14.95
12. POP/ROCK 00699587 .... $14.95	**31. CHRISTMAS HITS** 00699652 .... $14.95	**50. VAN HALEN 1978-1984** 00110269 .... $17.99	**72. ACOUSTIC '90s** 00699827 .... $14.95
13. FOLK ROCK 00699581 .... $15.99	**32. THE OFFSPRING** 00699653 .... $14.95	**51. ALTERNATIVE '90s** 00699727 .... $14.99	**73. BLUESY ROCK** 00699829 .... $16.99
14. BLUES ROCK 00699582 .... $16.95	**33. ACOUSTIC CLASSICS** 00699656 .... $16.95	**52. FUNK** 00699728 .... $14.95	**75. TOM PETTY** 00699882 .... $16.99
15. R&B 00699583 .... $16.99	**34. CLASSIC ROCK** 00699658 .... $16.95	**53. DISCO** 00699729 .... $14.99	**76. COUNTRY HITS** 00699884 .... $14.95
16. JAZZ 00699584 .... $15.95	**35. HAIR METAL** 00699660 .... $16.95	**54. HEAVY METAL** 00699730 .... $14.95	**77. BLUEGRASS** 00699910 .... $14.95
17. COUNTRY 00699588 .... $15.95	**36. SOUTHERN ROCK** 00699661 .... $16.95	**55. POP METAL** 00699731 .... $14.95	**78. NIRVANA** 00700132 .... $16.99
18. ACOUSTIC ROCK 00699577 .... $15.95	**37. ACOUSTIC METAL** 00699662 .... $22.99	**56. FOO FIGHTERS** 00699749 .... $15.99	**79. NEIL YOUNG** 00700133 .... $24.99
19. SOUL 00699578 .... $14.99	**38. BLUES** 00699663 .... $16.95	**58. BLINK-182** 00699772 .... $14.95	**80. ACOUSTIC ANTHOLOGY** 00700175 .... $19.99
20. ROCKABILLY 00699580 .... $14.95	**39. '80s METAL** 00699664 .... $16.99	**59. CHET ATKINS** 00702347 .... $16.99	**81. ROCK ANTHOLOGY** 00700176 .... $22.99
		60. 3 DOORS DOWN 00699774 .... $14.95	**82. EASY ROCK SONGS** 00700177 .... $12.99

83. THREE CHORD SONGS
00700178.............................$16.99

84. STEELY DAN
00700200.............................$16.99

85. THE POLICE
00700269.............................$16.99

86. BOSTON
00700465.............................$16.99

87. ACOUSTIC WOMEN
00700763.............................$14.99

88. GRUNGE
00700467.............................$16.99

89. REGGAE
00700468.............................$15.99

90. CLASSICAL POP
00700469.............................$14.99

91. BLUES INSTRUMENTALS
00700505.............................$14.99

92. EARLY ROCK INSTRUMENTALS
00700506.............................$14.99

93. ROCK INSTRUMENTALS
00700507.............................$16.99

94. SLOW BLUES
00700508.............................$16.99

95. BLUES CLASSICS
00700509.............................$14.99

96. THIRD DAY
00700560.............................$14.95

97. ROCK BAND
00700703.............................$14.99

98. ROCK BAND
00700704.............................$14.95

99. ZZ TOP
00700762.............................$16.99

100. B.B. KING
00700466.............................$16.99

101. SONGS FOR BEGINNERS
00701917.............................$14.99

102. CLASSIC PUNK
00700769.............................$14.99

103. SWITCHFOOT
00700773.............................$16.99

104. DUANE ALLMAN
00700846.............................$16.99

105. LATIN
00700939.............................$16.99

106. WEEZER
00700958.............................$14.99

107. CREAM
00701069.............................$16.99

108. THE WHO
00701053.............................$16.99

109. STEVE MILLER
00701054.............................$14.99

110. SLIDE GUITAR HITS
00701055.............................$16.99

111. JOHN MELLENCAMP
00701056.............................$14.99

112. QUEEN
00701052.............................$16.99

113. JIM CROCE
00701058.............................$15.99

114. BON JOVI
00701060.............................$14.99

115. JOHNNY CASH
00701070.............................$16.99

116. THE VENTURES
00701124.............................$14.99

117. BRAD PAISLEY
00701224.............................$16.99

118. ERIC JOHNSON
00701353.............................$16.99

119. AC/DC CLASSICS
00701356.............................$17.99

120. PROGRESSIVE ROCK
00701457.............................$14.99

121. U2
00701508.............................$16.99

122. CROSBY, STILLS & NASH
00701610.............................$16.99

123. LENNON & McCARTNEY ACOUSTIC
00701614.............................$16.99

125. JEFF BECK
00701687.............................$16.99

126. BOB MARLEY
00701701.............................$16.99

127. 1970s ROCK
00701739.............................$14.99

128. 1960s ROCK
00701740.............................$14.99

129. MEGADETH
00701741.............................$16.99

130. IRON MAIDEN
00701742.............................$17.99

131. 1990s ROCK
00701743.............................$14.99

132. COUNTRY ROCK
00701757.............................$15.99

133. TAYLOR SWIFT
00701894.............................$16.99

134. AVENGED SEVENFOLD
00701906.............................$16.99

136. GUITAR THEMES
00701922.............................$14.99

137. IRISH TUNES
00701966.............................$15.99

138. BLUEGRASS CLASSICS
00701967.............................$14.99

139. GARY MOORE
00702370.............................$16.99

140. MORE STEVIE RAY VAUGHAN
00702396.............................$17.99

141. ACOUSTIC HITS
00702401.............................$16.99

143. SLASH
00702425.............................$19.99

144. DJANGO REINHARDT
00702531.............................$16.99

145. DEF LEPPARD
00702532.............................$16.99

146. ROBERT JOHNSON
00702533.............................$16.99

147. SIMON & GARFUNKEL
14041591.............................$16.99

148. BOB DYLAN
14041592.............................$16.99

149. AC/DC HITS
14041593.............................$17.99

150. ZAKK WYLDE
02501717.............................$16.99

152. JOE BONAMASSA
02501751.............................$19.99

153. RED HOT CHILI PEPPERS
00702990.............................$19.99

155. ERIC CLAPTON – FROM THE ALBUM *UNPLUGGED*
00703085.............................$16.99

156. SLAYER
00703770.............................$17.99

157. FLEETWOOD MAC
00101382.............................$16.99

158. ULTIMATE CHRISTMAS
00101889.............................$14.99

159. WES MONTGOMERY
00102593.............................$19.99

160. T-BONE WALKER
00102641.............................$16.99

161. THE EAGLES – ACOUSTIC
00102659.............................$17.99

162. THE EAGLES HITS
00102667.............................$17.99

163. PANTERA
00103036.............................$17.99

164. VAN HALEN 1986-1995
00110270.............................$17.99

166. MODERN BLUES
00700764.............................$16.99

167. DREAM THEATER
00111938.............................$24.99

168. KISS
00113421.............................$16.99

169. TAYLOR SWIFT
00115982.............................$16.99

170. THREE DAYS GRACE
00117337.............................$16.99

171. JAMES BROWN
00117420.............................$16.99

173. TRANS-SIBERIAN ORCHESTRA
00119907.............................$19.99

174. SCORPIONS
00122119.............................$16.99

175. MICHAEL SCHENKER
00122127.............................$16.99

176. BLUES BREAKERS WITH JOHN MAYALL & ERIC CLAPTON
00122132.............................$19.99

177. ALBERT KING
00123271.............................$16.99

178. JASON MRAZ
00124165.............................$17.99

179. RAMONES
00127073.............................$16.99

180. BRUNO MARS
00129706.............................$16.99

181. JACK JOHNSON
00129854.............................$16.99

182. SOUNDGARDEN
00138161.............................$17.99

183. BUDDY GUY
00138240.............................$17.99

184. KENNY WAYNE SHEPHERD
00138258.............................$17.99

185. JOE SATRIANI
00139457.............................$17.99

186. GRATEFUL DEAD
00139459.............................$17.99

187. JOHN DENVER
00140839.............................$17.99

189. JOHN MAYER
00144350.............................$17.99

HAL•LEONARD® CORPORATION
7777 W. BLUEMOUND RD. P.O. BOX 13819 MILWAUKEE, WI 53213

For complete songlists, visit Hal Leonard online at
www.halleonard.com

Prices, contents, and availability subject to change without notice.

RECORDED VERSIONS®

The Best Note-For-Note Transcriptions Available

AUTHENTIC TRANSCRIPTIONS WITH NOTES AND TABLATURE

14037551	AC/DC – Backtracks	$32.99
00690178	Alice in Chains – Acoustic	$19.95
00694865	Alice in Chains – Dirt	$19.95
00690958	Duane Allman Guitar Anthology	$24.99
00694932	Allman Brothers Band – Volume 1	$24.95
00694933	Allman Brothers Band – Volume 2	$24.95
00694934	Allman Brothers Band – Volume 3	$24.95
00123558	Arctic Monkeys – AM	$22.99
00690609	Audioslave	$19.95
00690820	Avenged Sevenfold – City of Evil	$24.95
00691065	Avenged Sevenfold – Waking the Fallen	$22.99
00123140	The Avett Brothers Guitar Collection	$22.99
00690503	Beach Boys – Very Best of	$19.95
00690489	Beatles – 1	$24.99
00694832	Beatles – For Acoustic Guitar	$22.99
00691014	Beatles Rock Band	$34.99
00694914	Beatles – Rubber Soul	$22.99
00694863	Beatles – Sgt. Pepper's Lonely Hearts Club Band	$22.99
00110193	Beatles – Tomorrow Never Knows	$22.99
00690110	Beatles – White Album (Book 1)	$19.95
00691043	Jeff Beck – Wired	$19.99
00692385	Chuck Berry	$22.99
00690835	Billy Talent	$19.95
00147787	Best of the Black Crowes	$19.99
00690901	Best of Black Sabbath	$19.95
14042759	Black Sabbath – 13	$19.99
00690831	blink-182 – Greatest Hits	$19.95
00148544	Michael Bloomfield Guitar Anthology	$24.99
00158600	Joe Bonamassa – Blues of Desperation	$22.99
00690913	Boston	$19.95
00690491	David Bowie – Best of	$19.95
00690873	Breaking Benjamin – Phobia	$19.95
00141446	Best of Lenny Breau	$19.99
00690451	Jeff Buckley – Collection	$24.95
00690957	Bullet for My Valentine – Scream Aim Fire	$22.99
00691159	The Cars – Complete Greatest Hits	$22.99
00691079	Best of Johnny Cash	$22.99
00690590	Eric Clapton – Anthology	$29.95
00690415	Clapton Chronicles – Best of Eric Clapton	$18.95
00690936	Eric Clapton – Complete Clapton	$29.99
00694869	Eric Clapton – Unplugged	$22.95
00138731	Eric Clapton & Friends – The Breeze	$22.99
00690162	The Clash – Best of	$19.95
00101916	Eric Church – Chief	$22.99
00690828	Coheed & Cambria – Good Apollo I'm Burning Star, IV, Vol. 1: From Fear Through the Eyes of Madness	$19.95
00141704	Jesse Cook – Works Vol. 1	$19.99
00127184	Best of Robert Cray	$19.99
00690819	Creedence Clearwater Revival – Best of	$22.95
00690648	The Very Best of Jim Croce	$19.95
00690613	Crosby, Stills & Nash – Best of	$22.95
00691171	Cry of Love – Brother	$22.99
00690967	Death Cab for Cutie – Narrow Stairs	$22.99
00690289	Deep Purple – Best of	$19.99
00690784	Def Leppard – Best of	$22.99
00692240	Bo Diddley	$19.99
00122443	Dream Theater	$24.99
14041903	Bob Dylan for Guitar Tab	$19.99
00139220	Tommy Emmanuel – Little by Little	$24.99
00691186	Evanescence	$22.99
00691181	Five Finger Death Punch – American Capitalist	$22.99
00690664	Fleetwood Mac – Best of	$19.95
00690870	Flyleaf	$19.95
00690808	Foo Fighters – In Your Honor	$19.95
00691115	Foo Fighters – Wasting Light	$22.99
00690805	Robben Ford – Best of	$22.99
00120220	Robben Ford – Guitar Anthology	$24.99
00694920	Free – Best of	$19.95

00690943	The Goo Goo Dolls – Greatest Hits Volume 1: The Singles	$22.95
00691190	Best of Peter Green	$19.99
00113073	Green Day – ¡Uno!	$21.99
00116846	Green Day – ¡Dos!	$21.99
00118259	Green Day – ¡Tré!	$21.99
00694854	Buddy Guy – Damn Right, I've Got the Blues	$19.95
00690840	Ben Harper – Both Sides of the Gun	$19.95
00694798	George Harrison – Anthology	$19.95
00690841	Scott Henderson – Blues Guitar Collection	$19.95
00692930	Jimi Hendrix – Are You Experienced?	$24.95
00692931	Jimi Hendrix – Axis: Bold As Love	$22.95
00692932	Jimi Hendrix – Electric Ladyland	$24.95
00690017	Jimi Hendrix – Live at Woodstock	$24.95
00690602	Jimi Hendrix – Smash Hits	$24.99
00119619	Jimi Hendrix – People, Hell and Angels	$22.99
00691152	West Coast Seattle Boy: The Jimi Hendrix Anthology	$29.99
00691332	Jimi Hendrix – Winterland (Highlights)	$22.99
00690793	John Lee Hooker Anthology	$24.99
00121961	Imagine Dragons – Night Visions	$22.99
00690688	Incubus – A Crow Left of the Murder	$19.95
00690790	Iron Maiden Anthology	$24.99
00690684	Jethro Tull – Aqualung	$19.95
00690814	John5 – Songs for Sanity	$19.95
00690751	John5 – Vertigo	$19.95
00122439	Jack Johnson – From Here to Now to You	$22.99
00690271	Robert Johnson – New Transcriptions	$24.95
00699131	Janis Joplin – Best of	$19.95
00690427	Judas Priest – Best of	$22.99
00120814	Killswitch Engage – Disarm the Descent	$22.99
00124869	Albert King with Stevie Ray Vaughan – In Session	$22.99
00694903	Kiss – Best of	$24.95
00690355	Kiss – Destroyer	$16.95
00690834	Lamb of God – Ashes of the Wake	$19.95
00690875	Lamb of God – Sacrament	$19.95
00114563	The Lumineers	$22.99
00690955	Lynyrd Skynyrd – All-Time Greatest Hits	$22.99
00694954	Lynyrd Skynyrd – New Best of	$19.95
00690754	Marilyn Manson – Lest We Forget	$19.95
00694956	Bob Marley – Legend	$19.95
00694945	Bob Marley – Songs of Freedom	$24.95
00139168	Pat Martino – Guitar Anthology	$24.99
00129105	John McLaughlin Guitar Tab Anthology	$24.99
00120080	Don McLean – Songbook	$19.95
00694951	Megadeth – Rust in Peace	$22.95
00691185	Megadeth – Th1rt3en	$22.99
00690951	Megadeth – United Abominations	$22.99
00690505	John Mellencamp – Guitar Collection	$19.95
00690646	Pat Metheny – One Quiet Night	$19.95
00690558	Pat Metheny – Trio: 99>00	$24.99
00118836	Pat Metheny – Unity Band	$22.99
00690040	Steve Miller Band – Young Hearts	$19.95
00119338	Ministry Guitar Tab Collection	$24.99
00102591	Wes Montgomery Guitar Anthology	$24.99
00691070	Mumford & Sons – Sigh No More	$22.99
00151195	Muse – Drones	$19.99
00694883	Nirvana – Nevermind	$19.95
00690026	Nirvana – Unplugged in New York	$19.95
00690807	The Offspring – Greatest Hits	$19.95
00694847	Ozzy Osbourne – Best of	$22.95
00690399	Ozzy Osbourne – Ozzman Cometh	$22.99
00690933	Best of Brad Paisley	$22.95
00690995	Brad Paisley – Play: The Guitar Album	$24.99
00694855	Pearl Jam – Ten	$22.99
00690439	A Perfect Circle – Mer De Noms	$19.95
00690499	Tom Petty – Definitive Guitar Collection	$19.95
00121933	Pink Floyd – Acoustic Guitar Collection	$22.99
00690428	Pink Floyd – Dark Side of the Moon	$19.95
00690789	Poison – Best of	$19.95
00694975	Queen – Greatest Hits	$24.95
00690670	Queensryche – Very Best of	$19.95
00109303	Radiohead Guitar Anthology	$24.99

00694910	Rage Against the Machine	$19.95
00119834	Rage Against the Machine – Guitar Anthology	$22.99
00690055	Red Hot Chili Peppers – Blood Sugar Sex Magik	$19.95
00690584	Red Hot Chili Peppers – By the Way	$19.95
00691166	Red Hot Chili Peppers – I'm with You	$22.99
00690852	Red Hot Chili Peppers –Stadium Arcadium	$24.95
00690511	Django Reinhardt – Definitive Collection	$19.95
00690779	Relient K – MMHMM	$19.95
14043417	Rodrigo y Gabriela – 9 Dead Alive	$19.99
00690631	Rolling Stones – Guitar Anthology	$27.99
00694976	Rolling Stones – Some Girls	$22.95
00690264	The Rolling Stones – Tattoo You	$19.95
00690685	David Lee Roth – Eat 'Em and Smile	$19.95
00690942	David Lee Roth and the Songs of Van Halen	$19.95
00151826	Royal Blood	$22.99
00690031	Santana's Greatest Hits	$19.95
00128870	Matt Schofield Guitar Tab Collection	$22.99
00690566	Scorpions – Best of	$22.99
00690604	Bob Seger – Guitar Collection	$22.99
00138870	Ed Sheeran – X	$19.99
00690803	Kenny Wayne Shepherd Band – Best of	$19.95
00151178	Kenny Wayne Shepherd – Ledbetter Heights (20th Anniversary Edition)	$19.99
00122218	Skillet – Rise	$22.99
00691114	Slash – Guitar Anthology	$24.99
00690813	Slayer – Guitar Collection	$19.95
00120004	Steely Dan – Best of	$24.95
00694921	Steppenwolf – Best of	$22.95
00690655	Mike Stern – Best of	$19.95
00690520	Styx Guitar Collection	$19.95
00120081	Sublime	$19.95
00120122	Sublime – 40oz. to Freedom	$19.95
00690767	Switchfoot – The Beautiful Letdown	$19.95
00690993	Taylor Swift – Fearless	$22.99
00142151	Taylor Swift – 1989	$22.99
00115957	Taylor Swift – Red	$21.99
00690531	System of a Down – Toxicity	$19.95
00694824	James Taylor – Best of	$17.99
00690871	Three Days Grace – One-X	$19.95
00150209	Trans-Siberian Orchestra Guitar Anthology	$19.99
00123862	Trivium – Vengeance Falls	$22.99
00690683	Robin Trower – Bridge of Sighs	$19.95
00660137	Steve Vai – Passion & Warfare	$24.99
00110385	Steve Vai – The Story of Light	$22.99
00690116	Stevie Ray Vaughan – Guitar Collection	$24.95
00660058	Stevie Ray Vaughan – Lightnin' Blues 1983-1987	$24.95
00694835	Stevie Ray Vaughan – The Sky Is Crying	$22.95
00690015	Stevie Ray Vaughan – Texas Flood	$19.95
00152161	Doc Watson – Guitar Anthology	$22.99
00690071	Weezer (The Blue Album)	$19.95
00690966	Weezer – (Red Album)	$19.99
00691941	The Who – Acoustic Guitar Collection	$22.99
00690447	The Who – Best of	$24.95
00122303	Yes Guitar Collection	$22.99
00690916	The Best of Dwight Yoakam	$19.95
00691020	Neil Young – After the Gold Rush	$22.99
00691019	Neil Young – Everybody Knows This Is Nowhere	$19.99
00691021	Neil Young – Harvest Moon	$22.99
00690905	Neil Young – Rust Never Sleeps	$19.99
00690623	Frank Zappa – Over-Nite Sensation	$22.99
00121684	ZZ Top – Early Classics	$24.99
00690589	ZZ Top Guitar Anthology	$24.95

Prices and availability subject to change without notice.
Some products may not be available outside the U.S.A.

0516